HELP for your Growing Homebased Business

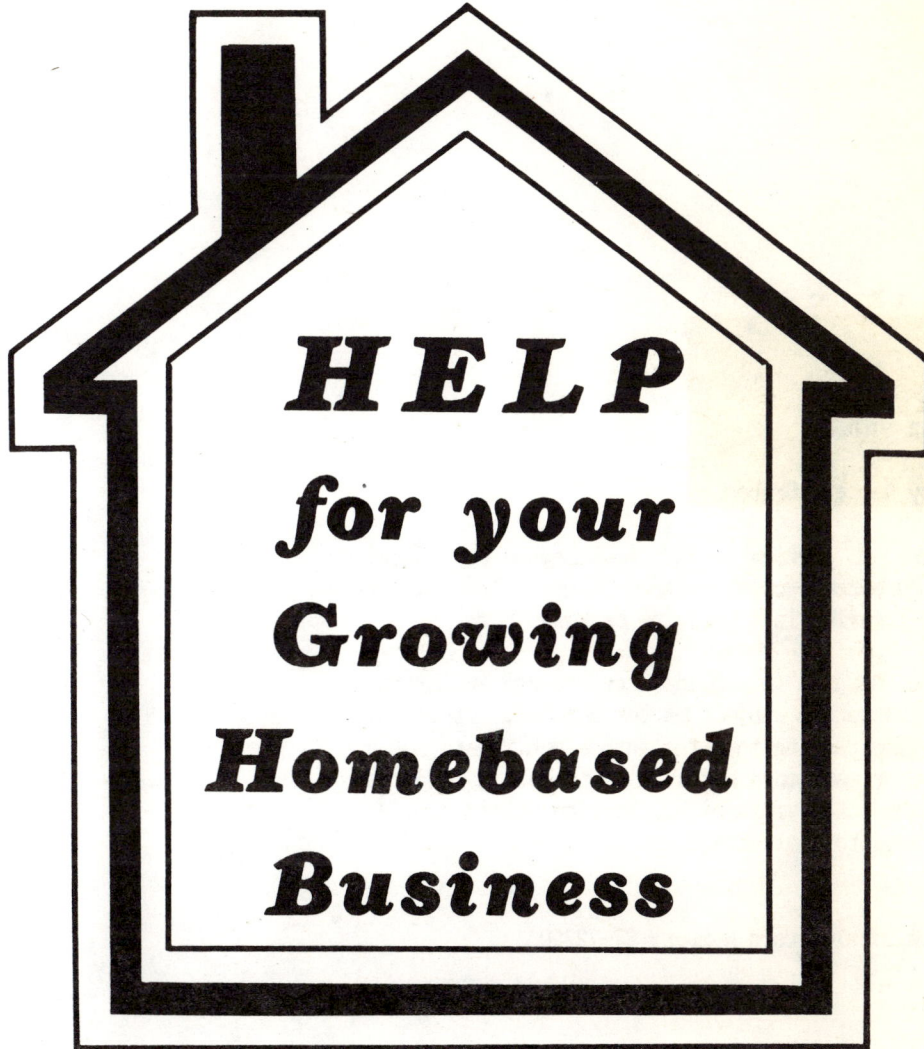

Barbara Brabec Productions
P.O. Box 2137
Naperville, IL 60567

Published by Barbara Brabec Productions
P. O. Box 2137
Naperville, IL 60567

Cover design by the author

This publication is designed to provide accurate and authoritative
information in regard to the subject matter covered. It is sold
with the understanding that neither the author/publisher, nor any
individual contributor mentioned herein, is engaged in rendering
legal, accounting, or other professional service unless
specifically indicated to that effect.

Library of Congress Catalog Card Number: 87-72260

ISBN 0-9613909-2-1

Printed in the United States of America

Table of Contents

Introduction

A reviewer has said of this book that it is "...*marvelously specific...the type of book you'll want to savor slowly, one page at a time. For serious seekers of homebased wisdom, the information contained in* HELP *is priceless.*"

That's true, and the reason is because this book reflects the experience and know-how of several small business authorities and homebased business owners in a variety of product and service businesses. Reading *HELP* is like sitting down with a group of special business friends to discuss problems one has encountered since the business began to roll. This is networking at its best—in printed form. In addition to getting some really practical business and marketing tips, you're going to learn how to avoid some pitfalls that could have cost you hundreds, even thousands of dollars in damages or lost business.

How did I amass all this great material, you may ask? Since 1981, my readers have been telling me what has worked for them and what hasn't. And I've been putting the best of this information and insight into my periodical, *National Home Business Report,** which also includes reports on what I have learned in the operation of my own full-time homebased publishing and mail order business.

So what you have here is the most timeless information from 16 issues of *NHBR* published between April, 1984 and January, 1987. The newsletter has continued, of course, and additional books of "*The Best of NHBR*" will no doubt follow because new readers are constantly discovering my newsletter, and expressing regret over the fact that back issues are not generally available.

If you find this book beneficial, a subscription would obviously be a wise investment. In addition to the contents of this book, as a subscriber to *NHBR* during 1984-1986 you would also have received a wealth of dated material, such as forthcoming events, timely marketing/PR opportunities, book reviews, limited money-saving offers on information resources, and material from such regular departments as "Computertalk," "Self-Publisher's World," "Book Reviews," "Home-Business Profiles," and "Potpourri."

---

*In the beginning, this periodical was known as *Sharing Barbara's Mail* and slanted to craft businesses only. The best information from these issues has been included in another book, *Crafts Marketing Success Secrets.*

You might find it interesting to know that most of the material in this book came to me in the form of letters from my subscribers and other readers who were responding to something in my periodical, or to one of my books. Articles from *NHBR* are presented in a different format from letters, as you will see. (Naturally, such material has been reprinted with permission and appropriate credit, and authors had the opportunity to bring their articles up to date.)

Letters, on the other hand, have been presented anonymously in most cases because it was difficult for me to contact so many people for reprint permission; and in truth, the sender's name is nothing the average reader needs to know anyway. The contributors of these letters did receive acknowledgment in my periodical and know, I'm sure, how much I appreciated hearing from them originally. A special section in the Resource Chapter does list many of these contributors since they offer brochures or other information of possible interest to this book's readers. There you will also find information on my other books and the availability of a free descriptive catalog.

Since the proof of the pudding is in the eating, I know you're ready to get going. I hope this book will whet your appetite for more of the same, and that I'll soon be welcoming you to my newsletter readership.

Barbara

P.S. While this book can certainly stand on its own, it will have greater impact on your business if it is used in conjunction with my major home-business book, *Homemade Money—The Definitive Guide to Success in a Homebased Business.* (Over 50,000 copies in print). This book is available in libraries and bookstores, as well as by mail from me. (See page 120.)

Alone, *HELP* offers an invaluable collection of information and ideas from many business owners—myself included—who have learned from experience. As a companion to *Homemade Money*, however, it becomes one of the best "Home-Business Success Packages" available today.

HOW TO ORDER A COPY OF THIS BOOK

If by chance you have borrowed this book from a friend, or the library, and would like a copy for yourself, you may order one for $13.45 ppd. from Barbara Brabec Productions, P. O. Box 2137, Naperville, IL 60567.

Industry Perspective

1.

To gain perspective on how the home-business industry is growing, it is helpful to look back a couple of years to see what was being reported at that time. For example, in a March 1984 editorial in *In Business* magazine, editor Jerome Goldstein said:

"The people who now run a home-based business are taking a fresh look at themselves and their importance. There's a new perception of the value of being able to live and to work at home. Instead of being defensive and grudgingly explaining the location of the business, the `homers' are finding that others wish also to follow their lead."

This editorial also reported on a recent study made by AT&T, which revealed that ten million households were then engaged in a business—with 60% of those people being between the ages of 25 and 44, and most of them young males. (*In Business*, however, thought the male-female ratio was much closer to a 50/50 split.)

My own editorial comments in the May, 1984 issue of *National Home Business Report* (hereinafter to be referred to as *NHBR*) commented on the fact that the AT&T study, based on individuals who had business phones or answering machines at home, did not reflect the many businesses at home which had no need for business phones—including many craft and mail order businesses, freelance writers, and self-publishers. (In fact, in all my workshops to date, only a handful of homebased business owners have said they have business telephones.) Thus, I suggested, the AT&T figure of ten million homebased business people might be only the tip of the iceberg.

I added: "Regardless of the total number of home-business owners today, male or female, one thing is certain: We're entering a new era—a period in which homebased workers are going to be recognized as a vital part of America's economy. With this recognition will come new dignity that will enable leaders in our industry to get archaic/unfair laws changed."

That prophesy is now coming true. At the White House Conference on Small Business in August, 1986, the concerns of homebased business were high on the list of issues conference delegates sent to the President and Congress. (See sidebar, next page.)

(Illustration clipped from an SBA brochure for a series of home-business conferences.)

The White House Conference on Small Business

Homebased business issues were high on this conference's list of important issues.

In mid-August, 1986, 1715 delegates from all over the U.S. gathered in Washington, D.C. to argue for some 350 issues in 22 sections. "The result was a surprising degree of mutual attention, courtesy and cooperation," reported Marc Behr, one of four New Jersey elected delegates. "All the concerns were analyzed, distilled, combined and prioritized. By the final vote on August 20, homebased business was on the 'hit list' of the U.S. Chamber of Commerce, Small Business United, and the Small Business Legislative Council— plus the delegations of NJ, NY, PA, DE, NC, OH, MI, TX and CA."

Of sixty top issues sent to the President and Congress by conference delegates, 21 were homebased issues, including repeal of the "sweatshop law," passage of the Freedom of Workplace Act, and deletion of the "red flag" on Schedule C (IRS Form 1040). On the same day came the Labor Department's announcement about lighter regulations for the now-prohibited six homework industries (see Homemade Money for more on this topic).

"This was the culmination of a year's work," said Behr. "Homebased business is now a truly national issue. The 'Invisible Workforce' is not only visible, but is a potent political force."

Home Business Conferences

In September, 1984, *NHBR* reported on the growing awareness among state executives and legislators that small business is a major contributor to state economic development. At that time, the Office of Advocacy of the U.S. Small Business Administration (SBA) was diligently working to enhance this awareness by sponsoring annual small business conferences for state and local government officials.

More recently, the SBA has begun to devote special attention to homebased businesses, cosponsoring numerous home-business conferences and workshops across the country, often working with community colleges, organizations or Small Business Development Centers (an arm of the SBA).

For example, nearly 700 people attended the All Iowa Home Based Business Conference in Des Moines in March, 1986. Jan DeYoung, Training & Publications Manager for the Iowa Small Business Development Centers planned and coordinated this major event with support from the SBA, SBDC personnel, area community colleges and Pioneer Hi-Bred International, Inc., who provided financial assistance. (See sidebar material in this chapter).

Iowa was the first state to host a major conference of this nature; in fact, this conference became the role model for similar events in other states.

Kansas' first statewide conference on homebased business was held in September, 1986, drawing several hundred participants. And in St. Louis, Missouri in October of that same year, homebased business was the focus of one of five sessions titled Americans Creating Tomorrow—Entrepreneurship Forum '86. As a speaker and workshop leader for each of these events, I can attest to the fact that enthusiasm and support for the home-business industry is definitely growing.

In late 1986, the SBA announced that more than 900 homebased business people had attended their fall conference series. As a result, homebased business would continue to be the focus of a new nationwide series of conferences to be held in 1987, these to be jointly sponsored by the SBA, Safeguard Business Systems, USA, and The Travelers Companies. As this book went to press, conferences had been scheduled in Los Angeles, Boston, Syracuse, Chicago, and Missoula (MT).

Special Home Business Project in Massachusetts

A statewide home-business project got underway at the University of Massachusetts in July, 1985, when the Massachusetts Cooperative Extension Service (Division of Home Economics) sponsored a Home-Based Business Master Teacher Conference.

Seventy "master teachers" were specially selected by the Extension Service to help them promote and encourage the growth of home-based businesses in Massachusetts, especially those in home economics-related areas. These include family day care, sewing and related crafts, bed and breakfast businesses, and catering.

The week-long conference featured workshops by Extension Specialists and outside business authorities in many areas. As part of their conference package of information, all master teachers received a year's subscription to *National Home Business Report* and a copy of *Homemade Money*.

"The trend toward the establishment of homebased business is being fueled by the decline of traditional industries, sustained higher levels of unemployment, women's changing aspirations, and the desire of many parents to be at home with their young children," says Elsie B. Fetterman, assistant director of the Cooperative Extension Service of Home Economics, and acting head of the University of Massachusetts' division of home economics. Both the university and the extension service are trying to design new services to help homebased businesses. Fetterman believes that faculty members are now doing more than relaying useful technical information to their clients; they're starting to make a dent in the underground economy by showing people the benefits of declaring home-based business income."

By the way, you don't have to live in Massachusetts to receive help from the Cooperative Extension Service. Contact your county's extension office to connect with a small business specialist in your area.

Home Business Trends Reported in *NHBR* in 1985

Growth of Underground Economy. A CBS news broadcast in January, 1985 reported that an estimated $100 billion a year is not being paid in taxes, due to the rise of hidden small business income. Meanwhile, tax authority Doug Casey predicted in his newsletter that the biggest growth industry in the next 15 years will be the underground (cash—tax free) economy. He also warned against trying to avoid taxes through barter services.

Flea Markets—Big Bu$ine$$. The Sutton Family in Florida, publishers of *The National Flea Market Dealer*, reported on this growing industry, saying: "Every time a large flea market comes into being, many satellite industries spring up all around it. A number of people are employed, or self-employed, because of that flea market. Nationwide, billions of dollars in merchandise is being traded, bartered, and sold for cash in the flea markets and swap meets. The underground economy is slowly becoming greater than the `Aboveground.'"

Explosion of the Information Industry. According to a spokesman for Dun & Bradstreet, more than 15,000 articles have reportedly been written about the exploding information industry in the past five years, and this industry is expected to be the most dynamic sector of the U.S. economy in the 80s and 90s. Research has revealed six trends in this industry: telecommunications, software, personal computer, mainframes and data processing, on-line databases, and data security.

"Soft Skilled Entrepreneurs"

Among those likely to profit from the growth of the information industry are what author Steven Bennett calls "Soft-Skilled Entrepreneurs." In his book, *Playing Hard Ball With Soft Skills* (Bantam paperback, 1986), Bennett explains how people with non-technical skills can prosper in the high-tech world now emerging. There will be practically unlimited possibilities for making money by selling, compiling, retrieving and brokering information, he says.

"As the need for technical knowledge increase, so will the desire for nontechnical courses and programs. Those trained in teaching the humanities and those who have expertise in arts,

Homebased Businesses In Iowa

"The general downtrend in more traditional Iowa businesses has created an enormous interest in home-based business," says Jan DeYoung.

"Because these small businesses operate from their homes, gathering statistics on their numbers, products and services is difficult. But we estimate between 15,000–20,000 Iowans currently run businesses from their homes, and the figure is rising.

"There is a lot of interest from rural areas where people need businesses that offer income potential without the high overhead costs that typically come with storefront businesses. Others are parents who view home businesses as a way to earn money and still remain home with their young children. And, of course, there is also interest among out-of-work Iowans, including retirees who just plain can't find jobs in their immediate area."

Most people envision toys, candy and crafts when thinking about home businesses. But DeYoung points out that home businesses are also engaged in sophisticated computer programming, marketing of specialty farm products, business consulting, not to mention light industrial manufacturing and a lengthy list of service businesses. But even though the products and services offered by Iowa's home businesses are diverse, there are many common problems and opportunities that need to be addressed, including legal restrictions, image problems, and challenges in competitively pricing, packaging, and promoting their wares against mass-produced items."

crafts, and other forms of self expression stand on the threshold of a golden era," he adds.

Others will benefit, too, says the author, "including soft-skilled people in the area of personal health, leisure-related projects (travel, gourmet cooking), and other non-technical activities that make life more satisfying in the Techno Age."

Who are the people taking advantage of these Techno Age trends? Bennett says they're ordinary people who are attaining their unique financial life-style and career goals through unconventional approaches to business. "And in doing so," he says, "they've come to typify a new breed of winner: The Soft-Skilled Entrepreneur."

Anyone who's interested in reshaping and repackaging their research, communication and organization skills into a successful business package would benefit greatly from this exceptional book.

Home Business Surveys

Until recently, few home-business surveys have been conducted. In late 1985, however, *Family Circle* magazine published the results of a survey they had taken of 14,000 readers who answered a home-business questionnaire. Although respondents were interested in working at home, only 53 percent of them were making money at home at that time. Of these, most said they worked to earn supplemental income. Sixty-four percent said they contributed less than one-fourth of the total family income; all worked an average of 20 hours a week. A third of the women who worked at home cited isolation as a disadvantage; only a fourth of them said they used computer equipment. To the disappointment of many, no figures were given on the average income these women were earning from their homebased businesses.

In that same year, however, I conducted a small survey of my own, sending a brief questionnaire to my newsletter readers. More than 500 took the time to respond, giving their best estimates of gross earnings for the year ahead. Here is a breakdown of those income figures:

        43% - under $5,000
        15% - between $ 5,000 - $ 10,000
        25% - between $10,000 - $ 25,000
         8% - between $25,000 - $ 50,000
         2% - between $50,000 - $ 75,000
         2% - between $75,000 - $100,000
         3% - over $100,000
         2% - did not indicate an amount

A survey last year in two counties in Massachusetts yielded some interesting findings about homebased business owners which compared closely to figures gleaned from my own survey. This survey was conducted by Home Economics specialist Catharine Porter at the University of Massachusetts. She reported that of 180 homebased business respondents, 73% were female and 75% were married; 12% were single, 10% divorced, and 1% widowed. As to age of business owners, 14% were between 21-30; 41% were between the ages of 31-40; 21% between 41-50; 13% between 51-60, and 10% over 60.

Of the 500 home-business owners I surveyed, 93% were female, 69% were married, 3% single, 5% divorced, and 1% widowed. Age findings were: 6% under 30; 67% between 30-50; 26% between 50-65.

As to where my readers live, 48% reported living in an urban area, 20% checked rural, and the rest made no indication at all.

Statistics like these are interesting, but they prove little. As long as there is so little formal survey information to work with, the best most of us can do is make educated guesses as to how much the average homebusiness person earns a year, how old he or she is, and whether the homebased business is located in an urban or rural area.

Working at Home: Not For Everyone

In 1985, a nationwide survey of 701 "knowledge workers*" in large corporations revealed that, given the choice, only 7% would opt to work exclusively at home. Fifty-six percent said that, even if telecommunications technology made it possible, they would continue to go to the office every day. Another 36 percent said they wouldn't mind working half-time at home and half-time in an office.

What these figures boil down to is that a lot of people prefer to work for other people. More women than men, of course, opted for the part-time combination of home/office work, and the older the person who was surveyed, the more likely that person would prefer to stay in the office. Tradition, it seems, dies hard.

*This survey was conducted by Honeywell Technalysis, who defines "knowledge workers" as professionals and managers who spend a large part of their working day dealing with verbal or mathematical information.

Looking to the Future

In August, 1986, the SBA's Office of Advocacy highlighted some important trends and issues of interest to small business owners everywhere. The message was that things are changing, and smart business owners will have to change, too, if they plan to be in business when the year 2000 rolls around. Following are just four of the SBA's predictions:

1. Self-employment will grow more rapidly in the next 15 years than it has in the last 15 years. In 2000, small firms will produce a major share of the nation's goods and services—about 40 percent of the U.S. output.

2. The shift from an economy based on traditional industries (manufacturing and mining) to one based on services and information will continue through the end of the century.

3. A shorter work week will allow more leisure-time activities, and will increase the demand for leisure-related goods and services.

4. By 2000, investments in computers and robots are expected to more than double and will represent more than 19 percent of all investments made by business.

Home-Business Realities

2.

I receive a lot of fascinating mail because I've always encouraged my book and newsletter readers to write to me about their home-business problems, ambitions and accomplishments, while also sharing their private thoughts about working at home. By now, my long-time readers know that I won't violate their trust, and will cautiously use what they tell me in a way that will only help and encourage others. In fact, many of my regular readers now send yearly updates, giving me a unique perspective on what is happening in the lives of many home-business owners nationwide.

Of course it is almost always women who write—not men—even though I do have a sizable male readership. Through the years, in reading so many heartfelt letters from women, I've gotten the impression that many of them simply have no one else but me to talk to. Other women friends may have little understanding of what they're doing, or "where they're coming from," especially if they're not business-oriented, or if they're totally wrapped up in the lives of their husbands or children. And husbands may be too wrapped up in their own jobs or businesses to have the time or desire to talk business with their wives at day's end. And there is a certain kind of husband who simply doesn't care what his wife does while he's at work. It's "Have a nice day, dear," and "Don't forget to have dinner ready by six." It would never occur to this kind of male that his wife might like to have someone fix dinner for HER so she can attend to HER growing business. Finally, it is my opinion that some husbands may feel so threatened by their wives' successful businesses that they simply can't deal with the topic.

Consider this woman's remarks, for instance: " Although I have lip support from my husband, I don't feel I have his full backing. He seems to think of my efforts as 'merely a hobby,' no matter what I try. I think he is somewhat fearful that, if I were to become successful, I might become too independent and not need him any more. I wonder if other women have this problem and how they cope with it?"

Men who run businesses at home will never have the special kinds of problems that women do, simply because home has always been thought of as "woman's domain." Whenever a woman begins a business at home, most people (particularly her spouse) will automatically expect her to do everything at home she's always done, even though her business now may be occupying a full eight hours a day. And the older the couple when the business is begun, the greater the problem will be, in my opinion, because it's difficult to change life patterns so deeply ingrained.

Personal feelings aside, the other letters that appear in this chapter make it clear that men and women alike have similar problems and concerns when it comes to getting a new business off the ground. In particular, I know you'll appreciate the letters from the two Bobs who wrote after I challenged the males in my newsletter readership to voice their feelings and concerns. When I asked Bob Storey and Bob Prisby if I might include their original letters in this book, along with an update on what's happened to their businesses since then, they kindly gave their approval. (By the way, Bob Prisby got a good chuckle out of my choice of words, "letting their hair down." After I published his remarks, he sent a photo of himself to show why: he and Kojak have a lot in common.)

Not surprisingly, the article from the two Bobs prompted several letters from women. One who wrote summed up the feelings of many when she said: "The letters from the men in your network were refreshing because they were willing to admit how unsure of themselves they are. Any man who's doing what these two are doing has a lot of guts. Most of us home businesspeople are housewives with husbands who bring home paychecks. There is no way I could do what I'm doing if I had to hold down a full-time job outside my home. The fact that these guys are willing to talk about this in a we're-all-in-this-together attitude with a bunch of mostly women business owners shows me that they have come a long way toward overcoming society's obstacles. Now, just like everyone else, they must deal with the obstacles they place in front of themselves."

Five Years and You've Got it Made?

An established business owner sent this letter to the editor: "In a recent editorial, you said: 'You know what they say: If you can make it this far, you've got it made. It's only a matter of time until you also achieve the financial goals you're reaching for.'

"In theory this sounds good, but I think for someone who might just be starting out in business, it is misleading. A business goes through several stages. The first stage is when the business starts up; profits are not usually made in this stage. Then business grows and profit is made. In the third stage, business levels off and finally in the fourth stage, things are on the decline and the business may again see a decline in profits or no profits at all.

"Businesses as a rule go up and down. Just because we have lasted five years does not mean we have everything made. A business must grow and change if it is going to keep making money. Even then there are going to be times when profits are low or nonexistent.

"I guess the main point of all this is WORK. It takes work to make a business turn a profit. I know you know that, but someone just starting out may say, 'Well, if I make it five years, I can sit back and scrape in the money."

Editor' Response: A point well taken. You can't just "sit back." In fact, the longer you're in business, the *harder* you'll

In the Same Trenches

A determined woman in Georgia writes: "My homebased business, born five years ago, has hit some bumps along the way, but I'm absolutely certain that this is the direction I must go; for my own fulfillment, to support the financial and personal needs of my family, and to contribute in a specific way to my community."

"It is essential for me to seek positive reinforcement just now. Though my family and friends think what I'm doing is nice, there is a sense on my part that only those 'in the same trenches' can really understand why, 'with all your talent, education and drive' you don't get any one of several great jobs and have the security and benefits of a salary.

"YOU know why, don't you?"

find yourself working to just hold your position (in the face of rising costs, new competition, etc.), let alone make gains.

Nonetheless, I believe that anyone who can see the light at the end of the tunnel in that first five-year period may be on the road to success; but if things look bleak at this point, a retreat should be considered.

Regarding your fourth-stage remark, I don't believe this is true of all businesses. At least it isn't true of mine. I *do* agree that all businesses experience frequent, often crazy, ups and downs, but from experience I know that in every one of my past "down periods" I found myself working three times as hard (and thinking more creatively) to pull out of it; and each time this extra effort has taken me not just back to my earlier level, but beyond it. The year my business sees no profits will be the year I'm dead.

The Problem of Time

A publisher summed it up nicely when he said, "I guess the most frustrating part of starting a new business, when the things to do outnumber the heads and hands and dollars to do them with, is the need to do in series a number of tasks that should be done in parallel. There are so many programs I should be implementing NOW—but can't because I'm editing or publicizing or whatever—and I wonder when I will ever have the kind of coordinated, multi-faceted program I have in mind. All this wailing and gnashing of teeth isn't just an idle wallow...I'm leading up to something."

Anyone who reads *NHBR* regularly will see that its readership as a whole is leading up to something, and the same two problems are shared by everyone: too little money and not enough time. But neither problem is enough to stop the person who is determined to succeed, and sooner or later each of us finds our own way around both problems.

Often, we compensate for our lack of business capital by cleverly utilizing the media for publicity, enticing family and friends to help us at little or no pay, and by learning to do hundreds of "special jobs" ourselves. Fortunately, no matter what we need to know, there are many periodicals and books available that explain exactly how to do it, and those who study hardest will make the quickest gains.

But how do we beat the time problem? Since each of us has the same number of hours to spend each day, our goal must be to make every minute count, and as we're counting, we should also keep reflecting on what we've accomplished to date. In looking back to 1971, when I was totally involved in the publication of a crafts magazine, I can remember always saying, "...but there just isn't enough time to do it all!" Yet, when I see what I've accomplished in all those years since, I realize that I MUST have had enough time after all because I certainly got a lot of things done. Maybe not all as quickly as I would have liked, but done, nonetheless.

So maybe what we all have to do is change our attitude about time, quit complaining about never having enough of it, and just try to find more of it. How? We can get organized. Plan ahead. Learn to do two things at once. Study to improve skills and thus speed work processes. Move faster. Sleep less. In short, let's use what time we do have in the most productive way possible, and quit wasting time talking about our lack of time.

"I tend to be a workaholic," one woman writes. "It's easy to do when your studio is just upstairs—and then I feel very martyred about having no time for myself. I finally found a cartoon that really speaks to me.

"Broomhilda has been one of my favorites for a long time, and in this one, the vulture is berating Nerwin for being so lazy. Nerwin is relaxing under a tree. He replies: 'Well, why not? Life's not a suicide mission!'"

Adds another woman: "I'm beginning to REALLY understand the amount of time necessary in running a successful business, and it makes me nostalgic about the years I was able, despite diapers, housework and everything else, to sit down and read a book and write a letter all in the same afternoon."

On The Value of Time

If you had a bank account that credited your account each morning with $86,000, that carried over no balance from day to day, and that every evening cancelled whatever part of the amount you had failed to use during the day, what would you do?

The answer, of course, is that you'd draw out every cent. Well, you do have such a bank. Its name is time. Every morning it credits you with 86,000 seconds. Every night it cancels whatever portion you have failed to invest to good purposes. And each day it opens a new account for you.

If you fail to use the day's deposits, the loss is yours. There is no going back. There is no drawing against tomorrow. You must live in the present—on today's deposit.

To gain a proper concept of time is to understand that it represents opportunity. On her deathbed, Elizabeth, Queen of England, cried "Millions of money for an inch of time!" All the wealth of her great kingdom couldn't buy an additional second.

Such statements draw us to a glaring realization: We must achieve a proper value of time, those 86,000 seconds a day, to use well the gifts deposited to our account each day.

———————

When People Push You Too Hard

In your business, have you ever found yourself being pushed by your customers, clients, associates, family—whomever—to do more than you felt capable of doing under then-existing circumstances?

And upon *letting* yourself be pushed to your limits or beyond, were you satisfactorily rewarded in the end, either with heartfelt thanks or, more importantly, money?

Most people in business are likely to say yes to the first question and no to the second. Certainly that has often been my experience. It's no wonder, then, that I've become more hardnosed than I was in the early days of my business. Now, when I feel too pushed by others, I tend to rebel by simply pulling back. After all, I'm the one in charge of maintaining my personal well being, as you are in charge of maintaining yours. Weak-willed individuals may let others push them beyond their limits only to collapse in the end, with everyone losing in the bargain. To succeed in your own business, then, you must learn to balance the needs of those you are serving with the needs of yourself and your family.

There will always be those who are disappointed in you, who expect more than they're getting, or who are too impatient to wait for you to deliver whatever it is you're expected to deliver. I try to maintain a philosophical attitude about those who demand more of me than I can give. I hope you'll do the same.

TWO MALE HOME-BUSINESS OWNERS SPEAK UP!

More often than not, women are the ones who take the time to write the letters that fuel each issue of *NHBR*, sharing information and insight, voicing concerns, presenting problems that need solving.

But as the *NHBR* network grows, so grows its male readership and, one by one, the men are beginning to write. The following letters are from two fellows who decided to let their hair down and "tell it like it is." Meet Bob Storey from Seattle, and "Bush" Prisby from Pittsburgh. With a bit of encouragement, both will become excellent networkers. - Editor

Bob Storey begins: "You invited men to write, so here's my entry. My business, Together Products, requires sewing and related skills. I got into sewing because readymade won't fit, my arms are two inches longer than average, and I wanted better designs for backpacking and hiking. Most sewing courses in schools aren't useful to me because 90% of the material is for women's fashions—which isn't my thing.

"I operate out of the basement of my parents' house, which means I don't have to pay rent, but I have to do substantial repairs to keep the place from falling apart—quite a change from my high-rise job in 1980. It also means I'd have quite a job to do if I had to meet customers here...which is why I'm operating by mail for now.

"*Operating* is maybe not the word for spending thousands of dollars, doing so much homework, and not making a nickel. So far I've spent about $4500 on equipment (including an Olympia ES 105 typewriter, a new sewing machine, and a Bosch 1582 VS saw for cutting tabletops, etc.), so kindly don't print those silly stories about people who claim 'we started with $12 and made $244598759 in our first week.' They conveniently forget about the stuff they had to start with—the car, telephone, etc. Realistic figures would be useful.

"In my case, the $64,000 question is...*is this idea going to make money???* The answer is: (1) nobody knows; (2) it will if I believe in it 100%. I've invented lots of things and filed them away for lack of time to pursue them...and one of them might be a winner.

"I read the chapter on publicity in *Homemade Money* and gave myself a nasty tension headache! I think it was because I felt unready to have the public invading my house...which is not the way it really works. My business desperately needs publicity, so I'm going to do some homework and find ways to do what publicity I can handle.

"I don't object to working alone. I can see I'd be more efficient if I had another person to trade ideas and jobs with. I have not had much luck talking about my business with other people because it's so specialized, and let's face it, most people work for somebody else and can't understand. Often I've wished I had a spouse-type partner (one of those sales-oriented people who can smile while she talks, like they do on TV).

together products ⋈

"I've had very little boredom. For me, that was always part of working for others. But sometimes I get so frustrated I go outside and throw snowballs at the house, or take off my fur hat and throw it at the wall. I usually get up about six and work a couple of hours, doing housework or remodeling stuff to keep warm because it's so cold in here in the morning. Then I jog or exercise for about 45 minutes, then eat. (I often bake bread.) I do as much as I can by phone and mail to avoid driving my car, which I may never be able to replace. I set up my workspace so I can do some tasks sitting and some standing, which is better for my back. So I put in a reasonable number of hours, but it's mostly on my own schedule and I don't have to put up with a chain-smoking maniac boss fretting about how long I'm taking or how much I'm spending.

"One of the big blocks for me was the notion—which is 100% absurd—that I don't deserve success because of all the stupid things I've ever done. Yes, we need others' approval for many reasons, but dragging around yesterday's mistakes and using them as a reason not to do your best today is just plain stupid. Guilt is an emotion-backed demand that only creates suffering and prevents us from doing our best. It takes more than work to create the life we want—it takes letting go so we can start fresh. I tell myself I have a profitable business, regardless of ALL my past mistakes."

Whereas Bob Storey typed his letter in two columns on his printed letterhead (legal-size paper), Bob "Bush" Prisby used Eaton's bond and ornamented it with an original drawing—the penguin at right. His letter began, "...Random thoughts from one of your male subscribers." It was beautifully printed in lines as straight as a ruler.

"The penguin," he said, "is one of my woodcraft items. I've thought about doing pen and ink notecards on a lot of my products—mostly animals.

"FLASHBACK: In January, 1984, my fiance, Nancy and I started to plan an informal wedding and reception. It was to be personal and a reflection on us. We rented an old house in the park for the picnic-style reception, which we planned to decorate. To save money, we would make most things ourselves.

"At that time, I was working for a moving company, doing extensive traveling, and Nancy had (still has) a job in the city schools. Anyway, we grew dozens of potted plants to decorate the two porches and walkways, flowering hanging baskets, plants for all the tables, macramed all the hangers, did grapevine wreaths for the windows...and stenciled borders on 24 picnic-size tablecloths which we made from muslin. Neither of us had ever stenciled before--it was a lot of work for amateurs. But the point of this story is that it renewed my interest in art and in being creative—something that carrying furniture for over 6 years didn't offer.

"We married September 15th—it was perfect. I don't use that word often, though I strive for it in everything I do, which can be quite a burden.

"So, Nancy and I talked about it...starting a business, doing stenciling. I wrote for info on everything. We figured we'd start doing large tablecloths as they were such a hit with our guests. After receiving a stack of fabric samples, brochures and letters, we were talking about how we'd iron...and that was the end of it. To iron 24 tablecloths for our wedding was one thing, but to do it everyday until we could purchase a mangle? No way.

"Well, somewhere along the line, woodcraft ideas came in, and my moving job went out. I spent the winter unemployed, designing, researching constantly about wood.

"I'm creative, talented—I've got quality crafts and so on...but I don't really know what I'm doing. I feel I should be way ahead of where I am now, especially in the sales department. I have a hard time not coming up with new things to make, which throws my production off as now I've got another thing to mass produce. It does take some of the boredom out of things. (Sanding is by far the most boring thing I've ever done—even worse than carrying furniture.)

"I enjoy being my own boss, though I wish I'd give myself time off without guilt. I have trouble getting started in the morning, but more trouble stopping at night. I do not envy my wife having to listen to me when she comes home from work.

"I could not have done any of this without Nancy, who supports me 100%. She keeps me going. I want to succeed for her—I feel it's only a matter of time.

"I've learned a lot from the two small shows I've been in to date, and I will soon be exhibiting in larger, more *(continued, over)* professional shows. I feel I'm on the right track, and I'm proud of what I'm doing. Since seeing which items sell and which don't, I can now make better use of my time, and think about possibly shifting gears into specializing."

And there you have it — two interesting fellows who have committed themselves to succeeding in a homebased business, each with different dreams and goals, but each sharing similar problems and concerns.

Bush adds he's having trouble finding NICE craft shops, and wonders if he's being too picky. Bob asks, "If we are not getting the results we want, how do we tell if the problem is (a) our hangups, or (b) our ignorance?"

When I contacted both fellows a year and a half after they first wrote to me, Bob wrote to say that he had not made the progress in his business that he hoped to make, but had not given up his dream of independence through a business of his own.

One thing he did learn, he said, was that operating by mail wasn't the right answer for him. "One of my advisors said to spend more time meeting with real customers, and she was right. My last mail customer took twice as long to satisfy and he has not responded to my request for feedback, or paid his bill yet. My next project is to rearrange my workspace to accommodate customers on a by-appointment basis. Since my job skills are being computerized out of existence, a home-business income looks more needed than ever."

Bush responded with a package of photos and printed materials that illustrated the progress he'd made as both a craftsman and a businessman, though he admits to still being more interested in the art aspect of what he does than the business side.

"What I am attempting to do now is create pieces that look older than they really are," he wrote, "taking 'new ideas into the past.' Because these items require more time, my product line will have a higher price range, and my clientele will surely be changing.

"My miniature folkart pieces, as small as one inch long, comprised 50 percent of my total sales last year...and to think it all started with a handful of crude miniature weathervanes made as Christmas gifts. I had no intention at that time to really get into miniature production. I now have to do the bulk of my work with a magnifying lamp. I expect to have about three dozen different miniature items by year's end.

BOB 'BUSH' PRISBY

FOLK ART MINIATURES CARVINGS

"Sales for 1986 were up 95% over 1985, a large increase percentage-wise, but still below what I'd hoped for. It takes more than a quality product to get accepted in good shows, and non-acceptance equals zero sales.

"Prompted by your 'log book' article (see Chapter Three), I am now doing the same, for as far as I can tell, only one-third of my time last year was spent on actual production. This has to change if I am to grow financially. Proper planning of all other business activities should help. Hiring someone to help with production is out of the question (except for items which are wholesaled) because many of the show contracts state in one way or another that 'the participating artist must be the one who conceived the design of the work and executed the finished product.'

"For wholesale production of miniatures, I am now in the process of training my wife and brother to do certain steps. With additional labor, Prisby's Country Miniatures could become a profitable business."

Words of Advice to Others Just Starting

"If you have need for tools, machinery, etc., buy the best you can afford or, if possible, wait until you can afford the best. And buy extended warranties from place of purchase if possible. I have one of Craftsman's best bandsaws, but even it does not seem to be intended for day-in, day-out use. Starting with limited capital, I purchased equipment that didn't even last the first year. This ended up costing more than you would first think because without the equipment, production either slowed down drastically while things were done by hand, or stopped completely."

In summary, Bush has found himself moving in new directions this year. "After taking the initial risk of quitting my job in 1984 to do what I do now, these new risks seem small," he says. "And being in control—most of the time—I can keep the odds in my favor."

His odds for success look pretty good to me.

THE CHALLENGE OF WORKING AT HOME

Here, several readers share their feelings about the advantages and disadvantages of running a business at home. These comments are typical of many I receive in my daily mail. Although presented anonymously, they are from real people in my newsletter network. - Editor.

The Difference is Psychological

"Setting up, planning, organizing and financing a home business is no different than setting up, planning, organizing and financing any other business, writes a successful designer and mail order seller: What *is* different is what happens to you in the process, merely because you are setting up the business *in your home* The difference between setting up a *home* business, as opposed to an *away-from-home* business is psychological one.

"Home business owners lack legitimacy in the minds of 99% of the people they will be dealing with. And women start out with a double whammy. Not only do they lack legitimacy because they are women (you must really be a dud if you can't even get out of the home with your business), and, if they choose an area that has been traditionally dominated by women (such as dollmaking, for example), then they REALLY have to fight to prove they are businesspeople.

"*It takes a special person to run a business from the home. Not everyone can do it. Not all are able to adapt to the demands and the isolation. Not every family can adjust and not every home or business is suited to the arrangement.* But a lot of businesses could start out in the home. Why borrow $10,000 to begin a business in an office two miles across town when you can save that amount in the next three years by running it out of your basement? Then invest your own money in the office. It is certainly worth considering."

"It Was a Humbling Year"

After a particularly stressful year, a successful but exhausted newsletter editor included the following remarks in an editorial, neatly describing something that happens all too often to women who try to be "superwomen."

"After several years of life running smoothly, and my smugness about being able to handle homemaking, a writing/publishing career which requires much mail order detail work, a small local herbal wholesale business and nine gardens all by myself...last year seemed determined to prove me wrong. It was absolutely critical for me to become more of a mother, more of a daughter, more of a wife, and more of a friend than my work allowed time for. I foolishly kept lecture commitments I was unprepared form, my gardens were 'on their own' (disastrously), I had to abandon my herb business, my newsletters have been running late, and my new book is way behind schedule. It was, indeed, a 'humbling' year."

Adding to the Picture

The next five letters, from women in different states, add to the overall picture of what it's really like to run a homebased business.

"When I started my business, I was hoping to help pay off the ranch mortgage and build a house," writes Shirley, in Montana.

"But with the economy the way it has been, money has become an absolute necessity. I sometimes think of the ad, 'You've come a long way, baby.' It beats going to an office every day, but I find very little time for the little things in life. Here it is, Sunday, and I have been writing business letters all day. Now I have to stop and cook supper."

(Continued, over)

Adds Ruby, in Kansas: "Even if you don't have a family to care for, there are too many other obligations in this world that interrupt your creative juices just when they're flowing. I seem to get my best ideas while I'm in the middle of working on things for a show and rushing to meet deadlines.

"During the slower months, I do only what I have to do and the mental processes stay in slow gear. But when art fair/Christmas season comes and I have to work almost night and day, then the old thinker seems to shift into high gear. They say you get what you demand of yourself, and I guess that's true, for when I put it to work, it seems to keep on generating the ideas and enthusiasm. When I demand only routine work, that's all I get done."

Meanwhile, in Florida, Eve reflects, "I so wanted to grow in management in my profession in the postal service, but I have decided I have what it takes to be management, and that I should grow out of the post office and into my own business.

"The gratification is indeed ego, and satisfaction, and grit and hard work. The decisions, therefore, are mine, as well as the failures and the successes. I have honed the art of networking, and found I don't need to be phony—just confident and knowledgeable of my work."

"I'm a floral designer," says Roz in Michigan. "In answer to the question in *Homemade Money* about pitfalls and warnings to others, the answer is procrastination. I estimate that I'm at least a year behind myself, but I'm working on it.

"In my area, zoning is a problem. I'm leery of pushing too hard...you know, promo bud vases to local offices, discount coupons, freebies, etc. I've felt the resentment I generated at florist shows when it was discovered that I (ugh!) worked at home, and to alienate the 'professionals' could be risky. They feel threatened by those like me who don't have shops and high overhead. The fact is that their vindictiveness could shut me down.

"Regardless, I will one day find myself to be a VERY successful businesswoman—'successful' here meaning respected and well-paid. And, who knows, perhaps someday I'll be able to come out of the closet."

Naturally, everyone who starts a business at home does not stay in it forever, but a lot of people who cease one homebased business tend to start another in time. Writes Ramona in Minnesota: "I had a small homebased craft business for a couple of years, and from it, made enough to pay for my computer system. I operated out of a little room measuring 8x10 ft. When, after five years of marriage we found we were finally going to be parents, we decided I should quit the business. Besides, we needed 'the business room' for the baby's room. I'm glad I decided to quit the business when I did. But I am now studying to start again, and reviewing all the mistakes I made—mistakes I will undoubtedly make again, even though I know what to expect."

Spang Against the Wall

"You think you're going to be pushed right up against the wall; you can't see any way out, or any hope at all; you think you're gone—and then something you never counted on turns up; and, while maybe you never do get back to where you used to be, yet somehow you kind of squirm out of being right spang against the wall. You keep on going—maybe you can't go much, but you do go a little."

- *From* Alice Adams
by Booth Tarkington

PRIVATE THOUGHTS OF HOMEBASED WORKERS

The following comments from readers across the country may help you come to terms with your ambivalent feelings about working at home, or reinforce the positive feelings you already have. Certainly they will convince you that you are *not* alone.

But What Do You DO All Day?

● *CHICO, CA:* "Without the encouragement from you and your readers, I don't know if my business could have become a reality. Just knowing there are others out there all over America, staying up bleary-eyed half the night, gives me comfort. Maybe I'm crazy, but I'm absolutely driven to be a homeworker, proud of each small accomplishment...and I could NEVER work 9 to 5 again, no matter what. But I DO get aggravated by people who remark: '...It's just great that you stay at home with the kids, traditional home life, home business, etc., but what do you DO all day?'

"One acquaintance, after hearing me describe my goals in their simplest form said, 'Oh, well, that's nice, but I mean, what are you going to do, EVENTUALLY?' And the question I really hate is: 'Do you WORK...or just stay at home?'"

● *BETHLEHEM, PA:* "I just can't seem to convince people that I WORK. Even my husband. When people ask what we do, he tells them I stay at home with our son. I've been working at least eight hours a day for the past three months, preparing for my Christmas rush. This is NOT a hobby!"

● *SANTA MARIA, CA:* "One woman actually told me, 'You don't know how lucky you are to stay home and make your crafty things instead of working. I have to work 8 hours and then come home and cook dinner for the kids.' She chose the wrong day to comment, 'cause I told her (in rather frank terms), that SHE was the lucky one because she only had to work 8 hours instead of 12-18, and SHE didn't have to contend with people who dump their kids on her while she's trying to work."

Learning To Value Ourselves

● *FT. WORTH, TX:* "Women are conditioned to be helpful, giving, and far too ladylike to profit by it," writes a perceptive businesswoman. "Women tend to undervalue their time and work, to feel a warm glow within when they give it away, yet feel guilty when it comes to putting a price on it. Such attitudes can guarantee failure for women in business more surely than lack of capital or the rising cost of materials."

● *IOWA CITY, IA:* "Those of us who are attempting to support ourselves with our business must convince people (including ourselves) that we are professionals. We must make an honest appraisal of our expertise and the value of our services and learn not to feel guilty about expecting others to compensate us accordingly. I think this is probably the hardest part—at least for me. But after all, the services and materials we require to run our business are not being provided free of charge.

"The things that really keep me 'hanging in there' are: (1) my willingness to learn and study; (2) my willingness to make personal sacrifices, from a material standpoint (As Thoreau says, 'My greatest skill has been to want but little'), and (3) the tremendous sense of accomplishment I feel, knowing that everything I have achieved in my business has resulted from my own initiative and hard work."

● *WHEATRIDGE, CO:* "So often, women are instilled with the message that the return they get for their sweat and hard work is LOVE. Oh, how people love the lady who is superwoman! If we could EAT love, all of us superwomen out there wouldn't be so undernourished."

● *STODDARD, WI:* "Your comments about missing summer (October '83 editorial) really hit home. I've been working full time in my husband's office, taking care of our family, and doing my business at night. I don't see myself as 'superwoman' and I don't know if I can juggle everything and keep my enthusiasm and perspective. Keep your fingers crossed."

● **WARSAW, IN:** I'm not dreaming that I'll make a lot of money; of course, that would be nice. But that may not even be the point of all this. The self-fulfillment of 'I did it myself' is what a lot of us are really striving for.

"Wouldn't it be great if we all had someone to take our hand and say, 'This is what you should do—here are your contacts.' But anything worthwhile doesn't come easy. If it did, we'd all be on easy street."

● **PRINCETON, IN:** "I have realized that I am an important person and that I do have good ideas, and that I can do many things well. Also, just knowing that I CAN do them—whether I do them or not—has given me a new confidence in myself. I am less frantic about things, less pushed to do things for praise than for personal satisfaction. So far, my business is not the success I had hoped it would be, but we'll try harder and give it a little longer. I've decided that if you have the courage to change your newsletter, then I will have the courage to try some new things also."

Problems/Decisions

● **LYNCHBURG, VA:** "My anxiety has come mostly from not knowing exactly what to do and what direction to go. Getting over the anxiety and off my duff and to work is truly something I have to deal with. Another problem I'm encountering is the time I spend working alone. I miss the contact with other people while I work."

● **SONORA, CA:** "My biggest problem is actually my enthusiasm! I want to do everything and I'm talented in a lot of fields. So many options! (I'm not too modest about it.) I'm beginning to realize I have to focus on ONE promising area and stick to it." (*Ed. Note: This letter was signed "Breathlessly,".*)

And Still More Private Thoughts...

"I think the biggest problem with anyone getting a home business started is lack of confidence, the willingness to sacrifice time, and FEAR," writes a beginner striving for self sufficiency. "It does require a certain degree of dedication and not everyone is willing to pay the price. However, I am like so many others—fiercely independent—and I could never go back to working for someone else."

Adds a wife well on her way to success: "My husband isn't happy in his work, yet he won't consider joining me because it would be MY business, not his. I'm willing to share top billing, but I won't give it to him and take a secondary spot...so perhaps it is just as well that he is not really interested."

I chuckled when I read this comment from another reader whose husband hasn't yet caught on to what's happening in his house: "My husband has no idea how successful I'm going to be," she wrote. "He thinks this will never develop into anything. Boy is HE going to be surprised!"

Even with success, however, comes feelings of discouragement that are hard to understand. Consider these words, from a woman whose success is assured: "I know most people would say, what has she got to be discouraged about? Maybe it is the realization that, whatever you do, it is never going to be enough. Someone will always want more out of you."

"Remember, Ginger Rogers did everything Fred Astaire did, but she did it backwards and in high heels."

- Faith Whittlesey, White House Aid, on the challenge of being a woman on the president's staff

MOVING RIGHT ALONG!

Things We've Learned . . . Gains We've Made . . . Changes We're Making

The following comments from other women in the *NHBR* network paint a vivid portrait of what so many home-business owners are going through, whether male or female. I wish I had more letters from my male readers to balance the picture, but as I've said before, they're understandably reluctant to write. I suspect, though, that they might read the following remarks from their female counterparts and nod their head in agreement. – *Editor.*

"The pressure to grow is tremendous!" writes a toy designer. "Everyone thinks having a larger company is the answer to everything. In truth, you just trade one set of headaches for another. For many reasons, I don't intend to let my business get large. For one thing, I'd have to go head-to-head with the big stuffed animal manufacturers, and they have mass production down to a science. I'm always looking for ways that my small flexible structure gives me advantages over them. Also, I'm not a great employer; I'm too much of a perfectionist and I'm constantly changing and adding designs.

"This year I plan to continue improving quality and design, but limit the quantity of animals. I will be raising my prices slightly. (It hurts to think I'm pricing some of my animals above what some people can afford, but if I want to stay small and continue designing, I think that's the way I'll have to go.) I will still have a small bunch of flexible employees, but that's all. I know this will not make me rich, but it will keep the business fresh and fun and I know that's the only way I'll keep up the work involved."

A now-successful designer/manufacturer of children's garments sent the following letter just before she jumped into the "big time." Her comments are certainly optimistic, but you can almost feel the stress this move caused her:

"I have tripled my business but, because of the nature of my business and the length of the capital venture that I must put forth in the garment sector, I am forced to capitalize this thing, via the bank, almost 13 months in advance.

"By cutting expenses cleanly across the board, I am trying to suspend and reduce my cash out as quickly as you can say OVERHEAD.

"As you understand, I must conceptualize the designs, putting my workers out on a limb with first and second samples 7 months prior to market; come up with the show fee (around $2,000 per season); do the printing (another thousand dollars) eight weeks prior to the show; take in orders and finance the production for the four months, ship them, and then hopefully get paid within a semi-reasonable time, guarding against collection.

"So I'm calling myself the Chrysler Corporation AKA Lee Iacocco. I'll be in touch."

"Expansion sometimes is a frightening concept, says another reader, "but necessary if I want to expand as I do. My main concern this year (my third in business) is expansion through more contract hiring and through finding a good sales rep. I design and manufacture a line of soft sculpture items for both wholesale and retail markets. This year I'm diversifying by adding patterns and a line of silk-screened aprons and hoops.

"I guess the hardest part is letting go of having total control, but there's not enough hours in the day for that."

Hiring Help

In order to expand, the average business needs to hire help—one or more full-time employees or independent contractors. But built-in headaches come with both. See the legal chapter in this book for more information on this topic while keeping the following comments in mind.

Says a designer and manufacturer of soft sculpture wall hangings, kits and patterns: "Business has been great — doubling each year since we began in 1981, but manufacturing can be a constant ulcer.

"Right now, we have 30 contract workers and four of us in the office." (Her business, originally based at home, is now in separate quarters.) "Because we were unprepared for the tremendous response to our readymade Christmas line last season, we were unable to produce it all and had to cancel 25% of our orders. Since our items are seasonal, we must keep a great number of items in stock for a particular holiday season, plus get them shipped in plenty of time for the shops, department stores and catalog companies to move them before the holiday is over. It *is* a challenge!

"Also, trying to work with the whims, wants and wishes of independent contractors can be wearing. For example, our heavy production month is September, and this year, ALL our contractors were canning or had some other reason why they couldn't sew."

Adds another business owner who has hired her first homeworker: "This past year I finally realized that I'm actually losing money by not employing others. The first home-worker I hired has worked out well, and I'll probably hire others this year. After reaching the burnout stage last fall, I finally sat down and made several lists — where I'm going with the business, how to get there, and what needs to be done now. It was an extremely helpful exercise."

"I've learned by trial and error, but that's okay. Every time I find an obstacle, big or small, I learn, and I'll never do those adverse things again."

"Burnout"

Anyone who has run a homebased business for awhile knows that burnout is a real problem for many people, myself included. My present business is now more than six years old, and it is more stressful than anyone could imagine. Much of the stress, of course, is of my own making because I have a tendency to take on more work than I can handle. Why? Maybe it's because I got a late start as an entrepreneur and, at almost 50 as I write these words, I feel time running out. There is so much I want to accomplish in the next ten years.

Some of us have longer "breaking points" than others, but none of us are immune to burnout, nor can we push ourselves forever.

"Last year was an absolute disaster!" writes a woman who pushed herself too hard for too long. "I foolishly allowed my business to ruin my personal life. This year I've resolved to run my business, instead of letting my business run (ruin) me."

Many individuals have probably gone through an experience similar to this woman's burnout and rebuilding process. She explains:

"A new partnership with a shop owner, trade shows, classes, book-writing deadlines, new patterns to design, and problems in my personal life finally did me in. By November, friends and family were seriously questioning my sanity.

"By December, I never wanted to see another piece of yarn ever again. I came very close to running away from it all and going to work 9-to-5 at a 'real job.' I really think I would have quit if it hadn't been for a good friend who pointed out that I couldn't throw away four years of work and success simply because everything else in my life was falling apart.

"From somewhere, the strength and determination have resurfaced, and I've pulled my frame of mind together. For the first three weeks of January, I did a lot of mindless projects: filing, cleaning closets and drawers, a little knitting, and surprise—a little designing. It's all part of my 'fresh start' campaign, and also part of the slower pace I plan to maintain. I'm out of the shop, my ulcer is better, and my time is my own. My enthusiasm is returning, and the creative juices are flowing.

"If I learned anything last year, it is that I cannot do everything myself and expect to do all of it well. Being a perfectionist is both an advantage and disadvantage. You have to learn where to draw the line. I think I have finally figured that if I channel most of my energy into designing and get good help in other areas, that the overall quality (and quantity) level is higher than if I try to do it all myself. Despite some rather costly lessons last year, I do realize how lucky I am. I'm young, healthy, happy...and whatever I lack in talent and brains, I'll make up for in enthusiasm."

Burnout, then, is a common home-business "disease" that can be cured by pulling back on the reins. The more complex your business, however, the more difficult it will be to slow down, let alone stop for a breather.

THE UPS & DOWNS OF A BUSINESS AT HOME

by Barbara Winter

Barbara Winter—speaker, writer, training consultant and entrepreneur—has been described as "a one-woman inspiration show" and "a dynamic change agent." Here is an uplifting, behind-the-scenes-look into her home-business life.

Thomas Paine must have anticipated the self-employed when he wrote, "Those who would reap the blessings of freedom must be willing to undergo the fatigue of supporting it." Ten years go when I started my first homebased enterprise, I thought it would be temporary. A decade later, as I move the stack of papers to one side of the table so we can eat dinner, and look at my bed covered with manuscripts, I have a hard time believing that Diane Von Furstenberg and Laura Ashley were also once homebased entrepreneurs.

The clutter is a minor irritation compared with an experience I had recently. It nearly sent me hunting for office space. If you, too, combine a personal and professional life from the same space, you'll empathize completely.

I had just put the loveliest green beans on the stove to cook, and turned the burner to "high" to get them started. My phone rang and the caller turned out to be a prospective client. I immediately shifted gears and became my most professional self. Not only was she interested in the projects I suggested for her company, she recommended another company that was looking for training, too. In the midst of all this business, I glanced across the room and noticed that the burner was now red hot and the phone would not reach to the stove. I couldn't bring myself to interrupt the client, so I decided to let the beans burn. Moments later, I was horrified to hear my smoke alarm blaring ferociously as I attempted to bring the conversation to an end.

Fortunately, running a business from home isn't always so chaotic. However, if Alvin Toeffler's vision about a growing band of homebased entrepreneurs is accurate, dinners will be burning all over America.

As a seasoned veteran of this emerging lifestyle, I feel a responsibility to share some ideas I've discovered to help smooth the way.

There are two major pitfalls to homebased success. For starters, there can be endless distractions. Not a day passes when I don't think about Jessamyn West's confession: "When I'm writing a book, I never get out of bed because if I get out of bed I always see something that needs dusting." It took me ages to develop the discipline to ignore what needs dusting. Add to that the phone calls and friends dropping by to chat and you have a situation that can send you rushing to fill out a job application.

The problem can be handled rather easily—and needs to be right at the outset. Let your friends know that you're serious about the work you do at home and let them know when you're free for a talk. An answering machine or service can monitor your phone, freeing you to get on with your projects. One writer took to wearing a special hat to signal her family that she was not to be disturbed. Devise your own variation of a "Do Not Disturb" sign.

There is another darker problem lurking and everyone who starts a business at home faces it sooner or later. It is, paradoxically, the opposite side of chaos—loneliness. There's no gathering around the water cooler, no buddies to gossip with at lunch, no co-workers telling you the latest joke. It's just you...all by yourself. Sometimes it feels like everyone else is out playing ball while you're inside practicing the piano.

Having spent 80% of my time writing the past few months, I consider myself an expert at staying motivated without the stimulation of others. My typewriter *(continued, next page)* has a slight hum and I have found myself talking back to it more often than I care to admit. Sometimes I carry on imaginary conversations with the people whose pictures are on my desk. But those are emergency measures. Saner options are available to the homebased entrepreneur.

Despite all the ups and downs of running a business from home, many people who try it can't imagine working any other way. The rewards of freedom, satisfaction and growth are so great that they more than compensate for the slow times and the alone times. Even when my dinner's burning, I keep in front of me Jess Lair's description of Picasso. He said, "Picasso's life was just exactly what I'm working for in my own life. You couldn't tell Picasso's work from his play. One minute he would be playing with a painting. The next minute he would be playing with his kids. The next minute he would be playing with his wife. And then he would be drinking wine and then playing with his paintings. It was all just love, love of his wife, love of his family, love of his friends, love of his work. He just floated back and forth between his activities without any thought to there being a division or a gap."

Lovely picture, isn't it? And I'm just stubborn enough to believe it's possible.

Editor's note: Barbara J. Winter is the editor of Winning Ways News, a motivational newsletter which emphasizes personal growth and business how-to's. In addition, her popular seminar, WOMEN WHO WIN, is conducted throughout the country.

This article was excerpted by permission from Barbara's newsletter. See the Resource chapter for her address.

Artwork, left, is Barbara Winter's news-letter logo. Copyright by Barbara Winter.

Ah, those interruptions in a homebased business! Writes the owner of a personable tiger kitten: "He was playing around on the floor and found a tiny spring, got it in his mouth, crunched down and —'do-it-yourself-braces'! We couldn't pry that thing off, so nothing else to do but drop everything and go to the vet. With interruptions like this, no wonder I lose track of my time. But, family comes first...even an orange kitten named Maxwell."

Working Smarter 3.

Keeping a Time Log

All of us tend to moan about how time flies, and if you're like me, you often wonder what you've done with the time you had to spend. I did something about this problem in 1985 when I began to keep a daily diary of how I spend my working hours.

This took discipline, of course, and the only way I could even remember to log my time was to constantly have that diary in my sight—and in my way. Even now, it lays on the right-hand corner of my desk to remind me to log each day's working hours.

One thing I hoped to learn from this experiment was whether I was wasting my time by performing certain routine tasks or, for that matter, doing other jobs that might best be farmed out to independent contractors. Now, after more than two years of keeping a time record, the habit is ingrained, and I intend to continue my time logbook indefinitely. It's telling me a lot of interesting things.

I shared a recap of my 1985 time log with my newsletter readers, but instead of reprinting that information here, I'll simply tell you what I learned the first year. The average employed person who works a 40-hour week puts in 2,000 work hours a year (allowing a two-week vacation). When one works at home, work hours may run from early a.m. to late p.m., yet with normal home and family interruptions, one is lucky to end up with eight hours a day in which to conduct a full-time business. My time log proved that fact to me. I logged a total of 2,235 hours on the business (plus 5 full workshop days out of town) and felt as though I had worked around the clock all year long. In truth, however, I found that time *not* devoted to the business totaled the equivalent of 93 days—including normal days off plus lost time of all kinds.

Unlike employed workers, home-business owners must work irregular hours, and because they have to squeeze in work time whenever they can, they get the feeling that they're working all the time. After awhile, this can have a depressing effect on anyone. Therefore, you'll feel better about your business if you keep a true record of the time actually devoted to business. You may find that, for the hours you're expending, you're earning a better hourly wage than you thought. Or, you may find that you're wasting time on one facet of your business that isn't profitable. You can then take whatever steps are necessary to correct the situation.

Why Businesses Fail

"There are about 600,000 small business failures each year," says Max Fallek, president of the American Institute of Small Business (AISB).

"Statistics show that nine out of ten failures are caused by the manager's lack of knowledge and inexperience.

"There is a continuing upward trend toward entrepreneurship, and the need for management know-how will become greater than ever."

In studying how I'd used my time the first year, I began to see what I had to do to become more efficient. This was when I knew I could not long delay the purchase of a computer, for I found that management of my mail list was eating up 12% of my time, and handling my mail (including processing of subscriptions, renewals and routine address changes) was occupying another 20%.

I've had my computer system for only two months as I write these words, but already I'm seeing an enormous saving of time and an overall increase in productivity in both my writing time and management of my ever-growing mail list.

Shortly after I'd published my time log information, I received the article from William Atkinson that appears on the next page. He wrote to say that my article was right on the mark, adding that he only wished he had read it five years ago. Then he went on to explain exactly how his study of his working hours enabled him to double his income as a writer. His technique, applied to your business, might double your income, too.

No Jam This Year

As I said in an early issue of my periodical, "time expands to make room for all the things we want to do." With my busy schedule, I really don't have time to can and freeze fruits and vegetables...but each year I do because good food means a lot to both me and my husband. We work together in the kitchen as we do in our business, and usually find this project a welcome change from our daily business routine. One year, as Harry and I were arm-deep in a bushel of peaches, we received a letter from a publisher friend, Miriam Irwin, who explained why she no longer felt she had time to preserve raspberries.

"I began narrowing down my life in my mid-30s," she said. "I gave up Bridge, needlework and reading current novels to concentrate on writing and researching. "In my mid-40s, I planned my publishing company. I gave up even more things I love to do. I have zeroed in on the one thing that has become by now almost a passion: I absolutely LOVE publishing miniature books. It uses all my skills; all my talents, all my maturity, all my patience. This past year I have given up one more thing in order to buy time to pursue publishing.

"I have a raspberry patch, and last summer it occurred to me that if I didn't pick and preserve raspberries, I would gain three or four days a year. This is the second year I haven't given in to the raspberry urge; and would you believe I still have jam left from three years ago? This just shows that whatever I did, I did with great gusto—but it diverted precious time and I have the discipline now to NOT DO EVERYTHING. Of course, by next year I may be out of raspberry jam and feel entirely different about all this."

I suspect Miriam will eventually preserve more raspberries, just as I will continue to can fresh peaches and tomatoes, because fresh jam and peaches are special pleasures in life, and we just can't give up EVERYTHING for work and business, no matter how great our passion for it.

By the way, you'll find Miriam's address in the resource chapter if you'd like more information about her books."

KEEPING TRACK OF TIME DOUBLED MY INCOME!

by William Atkinson

After ten years of full-time writing, I have only recently learned the value of keeping track of my time, both in terms of the number of hours I put in a week *and* where that time goes. Not only has this habit given me a handle on how much I'm "worth" per hour, but it "keeps me honest" in terms of putting in enough time and not wasting the time that I do put in.

I try to write an average of 10 articles per week (formula articles that take about the same length of time to write). I broke the task down into 20 component parts (from locating leads, to calling people to interview, to writing the article, to editing and mailing) and assigned an average time to each task.

For instance, if I spend 8 hours in the library and locate 50 leads (which is average), it works out to about ten minutes per lead. Totalling up the times of the 20 component parts gave me a total of 210 minutes per article (roughly 3.5 hours). Thus, I found that it should take me about 35 hours a week to write my goal of 10 articles. After keeping track of my hours, I found I put in 38 hours, which was about right, taking into account interruptions (unexpected phone calls, etc.).

Since I know in advance how much I will earn for each article (which I calculated by dividing the number of pages each article is into the amount I earn), I was able to calculate my weekly earnings in advance. The breakdown is thus:

$30 per page x five pages per article
(average) = $150 per article x 10
articles = $1500 per week divided by
35 hours = $43 per hour.

Prior to putting these calculations to paper, you would not *believe* the number of financially disastrous projects I used to take on! I would always rationalize the time wasn't that important, that I should always be doing favors for everyone who wanted something written, that it would be fun if not profitable, etc. No more!

Now I have no qualms whatsoever about turning down projects, and I do it with regularity. Before performing my calculations, while I was *capable* of earning $1500 per week, I usually ended up averaging only about $700-$800 because of allowing so many unprofitable projects to interrupt the really profitable projects. The simple task of recording my time and the tasks performed in that time—in actuality—*doubled* my income overnight.

I highly recommend that your readers take the few moments it takes to take an accounting of their time, to find out where they are wasting time, what tasks can be combined, and where their most profitable projects lie. Most people will find they don't have to work any harder—just smarter.

Keeping track of hours also lets you know how many more hours you have to work each week to earn X-number of dollars more. Again, if you're worth $43 per hour, put in 38 hours a week, and want to earn an extra $200 some week, you should be able to do so by working 5 additional hours (total of 43).

Next to purchasing a word processor, keeping track of my hours by task was the smartest thing I've done in ten years of writing.

Editor's Note: Bill is a lot smarter than the average writer. He's also the author of **Working From Home—Is It For You** *(Dow Jones-Irwin). See the resource chapter for more information.*

Years ago, when I worked as a secretary for a large company, I recall that I often threw away envelopes and stationery that had typo errors on them. And I never gave it a thought. After all, what was one envelope or another letterhead in the scheme of things in the big business world? Paper clip hit the floor? Why bother to pick it up...the cleaning lady would find it, right?

Well, now that *I'm* paying for the envelopes, stationery and paper clips, I think twice before I throw them away. If I ruin one of my fancy letterheads, at least I cringe when I crumple it for the wastebasket, remembering that it cost me 13.4 cents to print.

Envelopes I would have tossed before are now saved by covering the incorrect address with a self-stick label. I use these to pay bills. And I pick up paper clips, too, because they're costly to replace (to say nothing of being hard on the vacuum sweeper when *this* cleaning lady runs it).

Of course, you become aware of things like this only when you make the effort to become cost conscious and unit-price oriented. See the card below? This year I took the time to set up a three-year history of previous printing costs, office supplies, and other materials used in the business.

ARTICLE				
71629				
DATE	QUANTITY	PRICE	PER	PURCHASED FROM

Now, when I order supplies or printing, I have a handy record not only of where I last got them, and when, but at what price. By checking my invoices against these cards, I can quickly spot billing errors when they occur. What I see on the card may prompt me to look for a new source of supply, or perhaps increase the size of certain orders to get a better discount.

By the way, do not include shipping costs in your per-unit figures as you'll want to compare "apples to apples" when comparing suppliers. Freight costs mount up, and you may get not only lower unit prices from some new supplier, but lower shipping costs as well if he's located nearer to you.

Once you become aware of unit costs, you'll tend to be more careful in ordering printed materials, I'm sure. If you need only 300 copies of a press release, for example, don't order 500 "to save money on quantity." After all, you've only lost the cost of the other 200 releases if you don't use them.

There is reverse logic here, too, as in the case of promotional materials. Once you know that your brochure costs only 15 cents, and you realize it could easily yield an order for $25 or more, you also realize the importance of getting as many of them into prospective customers' hands as possible.

Becoming unit-conscious in your business can result in increased profits at the end of the year. And whenever you see your suppliers increasing their prices, you ought to consider whether price increases are necessary in your own business.

So dig out those old paid bills and calculate the unit price of everything you've purchased in the recent past, be it raw materials, office supplies, printing, or goods for resale. Remember that small business owners cannot afford to waste any of their profits, and attention to the small details like this can often make a big difference.

Ten Steps to Greater Profits Every Year

While you're working to cut costs and increase profits, don't forget to make the necessary business and marketing plans you'll need for continued success in your growing business. You may have the edge on your market right now, but at any moment the competition could move in *en masse*. What do you do when you find yourself swimming upstream in the face of increasing competition and greater sales resistance on the part of buyers? The answer sounds simple, but it takes a lot of thought and effort: You've got to develop special strategies for growth and greater financial success. You'll get some help in this department in later chapters of this book, but for now, let me share with you the ten-point list I published last year after I found myself in this situation:

1. Remain consistent in the quality of your products and services.

2. Further develop your own special style of doing business. In the end, people do business with people — not "companies" or "businesses."

3. Size up your competition. Find their weak points and capitalize on them. Fight back with appropriate marketing strategies and sales pitches.

4. More sharply identify your niche in the business world, and your special customer prospects; then intensify your sales/marketing activities in this direction.

5. Enlist the aid of those who believe in you and what you are doing. Figure out ways in which you can work with others on a commission basis. Let them help you grow.

6. Get serious about managing your business. Make things happen by first making plans, then doing something about them.

7. Figure out how to add to your overall profits by adding new products or services.

On Naming a Product

Here's an exercise to help you name a new product. On a sheet of paper, set up four columns headed RANK, NAME, CONNOTES, and DENOTES.

Under RANK, list the names of your competitors and rank them in order of their importance in the industry.

For each company, write the NAME of the product they make that you think is competition for yours.

After each product name, jot down what you associate with each names (such as low cost, no mess, fast and easy, or perhaps nothing at all).

Finally, jot down whatever else the name means to you (cheap, expensive, good reputation, dependable, etc.)

Remember that a product name cannot connote or denote anything until publicity or advertising has accomplished some kind of name recognition. And before you waste your time and money trying to make your customer prospects notice your new product, make sure the name suggests to them exactly what you want it to.

As a further test, ask some of your friends and business acquaintances to tell you what your new product name suggests to them—before they've seen the product in question. Their response may amaze you...and send you straight back to the drawing board.

8. Keep looking for new ways to sell everything. The possibilities are enormous and often overlooked.

9. Study the financial figures of your business to pinpoint your strongest, most profitable products and services. Also look for ways to cut costs and increase profits.

10. If you do not always meet your financial goals, remember that you're doing fine when you can simply hold your position in the face of increasing competition. Longevity in one's business is an important success factor!

The Importance of Your Business Name

In the next article, you're going to get some good tips on how to name a business. Since most of you have probably named your business already, let me emphasize the importance of changing the name if it is inappropriate for any reason. The wrong name can automatically position you in the wrong market simply because it creates the illusion in buyers' minds that you're selling something other than what you actually offer.

I learned this lesson the hard way. My periodical was originally known as *Sharing Barbara's Mail*, a name that seemed perfectly logical to me at the time I began publishing. I was simply passing along information and advice contributed by my growing audience of book readers. The only problem was that I also attracted a lot of people who had never read my books, nor heard of me before. To such people, the name of my newsletter sounded like some kind of pen pal publication when in fact it was a crafts marketing newsletter of the highest quality.

I knew about this problem a long time before I did anything about it. Like everyone else, I resist change because it's easier to keep doing the same thing in the same old way. And it's cheaper, too. It takes time and money to make major changes in a business—to redesign printed materials, get out new publicity, and explain to your customers why things are changing.

I quickly learned, however, that it's a lot more expensive to keep the wrong name than it is to pay the price of a new one. After changing my periodical's name to *National Home Business Report* (and also increasing the subscription rate), my circulation increased dramatically because I no longer had to explain the name.

Prior to this repositioning move, I had used the business name of *Artisan Crafts*. This was no longer appropriate to a publication that had expanded to include all homebased businesses, so I changed it to *Barbara Brabec Productions*, which suggests I'm involved in a number of activities. (And besides, I tend to make a production of everything I do.) Since I've been promoting my name since 1971, it seemed only logical to continue to build on this solid base. It was a wise decision.

I may be the only Barbara Brabec in my field, but since I've been in business, two women with the same name have written to inquire if I might be a lost relation (I wasn't). I learned about a third woman when we moved back to the Chicago area in 1984. A friend had tried to get my phone number and ended up talking to someone in Evanston, Illinois, who claimed to be the real Barbara Brabec; I must be an imposter, she said.

NAMING THE BABY *(Uh, The Business)*

by Janet Oberndorfer

One essential consideration which is almost never addressed in seminars on starting a business is how to select a name for it.

Now you may wonder why this is important at all; you may plan to use your own name, of which you are justifiably proud. Indeed, you may feel this is not an issue at all, for precisely the reason that you *are* going to use your own name.

There are times, however, when it is not always useful to use your given name. Here are some examples:

● When your name is Janet Oberndorfer, or any similar kind of multi-syllabic appellation.

Using, spelling, or pronouncing your name correctly is a mark of respect, and since those approaching you don't want to commit the *faux pas* of misuse, it may be easier for them if you have chosen an entirely different name. My name, Janet Oberndorfer, is me. There is no one who is more proud of her name than I am of mine. It is at once the least I have, and *everything* I have. But, I also know from several decades of experience that it is enough of a tongue-twister that I want to make it the easiest for people to contact me. There will always be someone who would be intimidated by all the letters—and won't even pick up the 'phone. It is for such as those that I chose an entirely different name for my business. I chose *Lady Resourceful.*

● You may wish to use another name when you wish to be intentionally vague about your functions, or when you wish to get past mis-perceptions immediately, so you can get down to business at once. I am a Home Economist. "A teacher," you might say, "like Mrs. Ogilvie in the 7th grade, right?" Wrong!

I am a business Home Economist. Primarily I do recipe development, demonstrations, style food for photography, write, work with advertising agencies and the electronic media, perform consumer analysis and publicity—a wide range of marketing and promotion functions. My corporate name, Lady Resourceful, doesn't say this at all...then again, it does — just not specifically.

● You may wish to use another name when you wish to *exceed* the perceptions of those approaching you. Sherlock Holmes, Private Detective, presents a rather focused picture of Holmes' services. In my own case, the name Lady Resourceful is broad enough to accommodate corporate growth, bringing with it the inclusion of additional divisions. The Sales Division distributes premium merchandise appropriate to industry categories previously mentioned. Grow & Go'™ the Seminar Division, provides training tailored to women, including "How to Start Your Own Business," and "How to Name Your Company."

Whatever name you do choose, remember it should bear some relation to what work you will be doing. Before I settled on Lady Resourceful, I had seriously considered "Dogwood Associates." After all, I reasoned, a dogwood is beautiful like a woman and, although the blossoms are delicate (it being a tree), it has strength. I am a woman and I have strength. It has branches as I will have corporate divisions. I thought it was a perfect name and I rushed to tell my graphic artist who was waiting to set type.

She said she thought it was a nice name and added, "Why don't you think about it over the weekend." Luckily, I did. Sometime later after Lady Resourceful had been adopted, she confided to me she was so glad that I had not chosen Dogwood Associates. "After all," she said, "you're not a gardener."

Big or small, handsome or plain, names are like people. Some will be remembered and some will not. And you don't want the latter to befall you. Keep in mind that your name should work for you. Your goal in selecting a name should be to create the image you wish to convey, and to correctly position yourself in your market. Your name can become a powerful marketing tool supporting and enhancing your (other) daily business activities.

Choosing a name requires a careful, organized, and scientific thought process. Done slowly and methodically, this will enable you to choose one to serve your needs, have memorability, unique character or identity, and even be legally protected.

Good luck!

Editor's Note: Janet Oberndorfer is available as a speaker and to present seminars for groups. See the Resource Chapter for more information.

Sole Proprietorships: A Double-Edged Sword

When a publisher friend of mine ceased publication of her periodical, she wasn't prepared for the volume of mail she received from caring subscribers and friends. So many anguished letters—thousands of them, in fact.

"Do you budget postage for closing a business, especially when you're already in debt? Are you obliged to answer all the letters?" she asked, pointing out that this is a problem no one has addressed in the small business books to date.

She's right. All of us who have written how-to books have been so concerned with *starting* a business that we've forgotten that all things must end sometime. When you assume the obligation of starting a sole proprietorship, you automatically assume the obligation of someday stopping that business as well.

Truly, a sole proprietorship is a double-edged sword in that one usually has little money with which to start, and even less when the business must cease because of lack of profit. While partnerships and corporations may continue merrily on their way without you, what happens if you decide to stop the business that is owned and operated by you alone?

Two kinds of businesses suffer most: publishing and mail-order. That's because the mail never stops coming, especially if you've done a good job with your advertising and publicity. People will continue to send you money for your products and publications for YEARS after you've ceased business. And this mail has to be answered. There will also be letters of inquiry from people who want your brochure, catalog, or whatever else you were advertising.

So what's the solution, if any? I suppose some people who want to escape a business and its obligations will simply move or close their post office box without leaving a forwarding address. This, at least, will get the mail returned to senders. But this is definitely the coward's way out, and a sure way to ruin the business reputation an individual has fought so hard to achieve.

My own solution to this problem when we let *Artisan Crafts* go out of print in late 1976 was easy because I still had something to sell. Only magazine reprints and a few books, of course, but something. All I had to do was create a new brochure explaining what had happened, and enclose it with my replies to mail. This kind of feedback business didn't make much money, but it definitely offset my costs in answering mail until I was ready to move in a new direction.

My publisher friend has decided to answer all her mail, too, because she may want to do business with the same people again. Besides, she says, "I care about them." But multiply 22 cents times several thousand letters, and you can see that we're talking big bucks here.

Any business that generates mail should send a press release to periodicals in its field at the time business ceases. This will help stem the flow of inquiries and orders resulting from earlier advertising and publicity in the same publications. Periodical publishers are also advised to put a large notice in their last issue which clearly explains that reader mail can't be answered without a self-addressed, stamped envelope (SASE). (People will still write and not send the SASE, but at least you won't feel as guilty about not responding.)

A few well-placed letters to special people in your business network are also called for, especially if you're looking for support for a new endeavor you're planning.

As a sole proprietor who's just on the brink of success, with many exciting years of good business ahead, it may seem ridiculous to think now about how you're going to get OUT of the business you're working so hard to build. But take it from one who's been there: It's a kind of insurance to know where the exit is. Remember my business motto: "Hope for the best...prepare for the worst...and always leave yourself an escape route."

Insurance Lessons Learned the Hard Way

Speaking of insurance, I learned some hard insurance lessons in the past two years that may benefit you. First, a few words about medical insurance.

Without question, the best bet for self-employed individuals is to join an organization that offers a comprehensive plan...but take a tip from me and make sure the organization you join is both large and long-established.

When I started my business, I joined a prestigious writer's organization primarily to get the benefit of their then excellent and low-cost million-dollar major medical plan. To my dismay, however, premiums that began at about $1800 a year have now increased to over $5,000 a year.

Upon questioning these ever-increasing rates, I was told that one reason was because the writer's organization was small (only about 600 members) and they were also putting in a lot of claims, a factor that automatically increases premium rates of any group.

Furthermore, Harry and I were forced to buy a family plan and pay premiums for non-existing children. The last increase of $35/month was for a drug prescription service we neither need nor want, yet it's not an optional choice. The crowning blow came when the rates increased and our benefits declined; specifically, they raised the deductible and cut our hospitalization coverage from 100 percent to 75 percent—a factor that could destroy our savings in the event of a medical disaster such as cancer.

In view of the above, we made application to a plan offered by The National Association for the Self-Employed, which I recommend in spite of the fact that we were denied coverage due to pre-existing conditions.

Following are some things the insurance agent reminded me to look for while shopping for a new medical plan. Ideally, you want:

- a choice of deductibles
- a stop-loss feature that limits your financial risk
- a plan that doesn't charge for children if you don't have them
- sufficient outpatient coverage for such things as cancer treatment
- benefits that cover organ transplants/implants

By the way, most policies do not cover the latter item, and many severely limit the dollar amount of outpatient treatment benefits, so check these points carefully. They're the ones that could bankrupt you if the worst should happen. *(The NASE plan mentioned above does offer these benefits.)*

Update to Info at Left

On May 6, we received notice that our medical insurance was being cancelled due to too many claims being entered by the group through which we were insured. This news came as a terrible shock, and as luck would have it, Harry had to have open heart surgery before the month of May ended.

We were offered a conversion policy, but it covers hospitalization costs only; we lost all our major medical coverage at a time when we needed it most to cover follow-up doctor visits, special heart exercise classes, etc.

We are now uninsurable as a result of even more pre-existing conditions, and feel very betrayed, both by the organization that insured us and assured us that such a thing would never happen, and by Blue Cross, which would not automatically convert our major medical policy along with the hospitalization insurance.

All the more reason for this book's readers to be concerned about their medical insurance policies. Make sure you read the fine print about cancellation conditions, conversion privileges, and disability clauses, and upgrade your insurance if at all possible. Surprise medical expenses are the last thing a self-employed individual needs.

Also, if you obtain insurance that covers your spouse, ask what will happen in the event of your untimely death. Will your spouse be able to continue the insurance at similar premium rates, and get similar benefits? (Not usually the case with most employee policies.)

Above all, check the size of the insured membership. NASE, for example, has over 100,000 members and an insured base much greater than that due to employees in this program. Interestingly, NASE won't accept any self-employed person with more than four employees. They say their company has a lower-than-usual percentage of claims entered, and they're convinced it's because most self-employed individuals simply can't afford to get sick. This psychological factor actually helps them stay well, NASE maintains.

See the Resource Chapter for the address of this organization. I'm told that 95% of those who join do so specifically for the insurance coverage alone; however, membership does bring a number of other moneysaving benefits, particularly to those who travel.

Homeowner's Insurance Pitfalls

Take time now to reread the fine print in your homeowner's insurance policy to make sure you're covered for such things as sewer backup, sump pump failure, and storm damage. As one of my readers reported, losses can be expensive without them. She wrote after Hurricane Gloria had devastated her area:

"The hurricane disrupted the budding business I'm trying to get going, and a lot of our losses are not covered by insurance," she reported. "Major damage was by water and falling trees across power lines and roadways. We did not have power for ten days. These items are not covered by insurance unless the water came in a hole caused by the storm, or the trees hit the house."

Another reader took time to send this note after a fire destroyed the historic building that housed her weaving store and family: "The building, all our clothing, furniture and personal items were a total loss. My store had a 3-1/2 foot wall dividing it from the living space, and most of these items were ozoned, cleaned, and sold at 75-90% off. I had a wonderful supplier who extended credit so I could restock in a temporary location. But the point I would like to make is INSURANCE. Contrary to what our agent had told us, none of my business items were covered (about $40,000 in stock)."

Again, let me emphasize the importance of having either a special business rider on your home insurance policy, or a separate business insurance policy. One thing I learned later than I should have was that the business rider attached to our house policy (which insures items on replacement at actual cost, not depreciated values) does not fall under this replacement cost feature of the insurance. In other words, in case of loss, our house furnishings would be replaced at cost, whereas the desk in my office would be calculated based on depreciated value. That's one good reason to have your computer system insured separately as business equipment.

Other thoughts: Make sure your insurance is of the "all risk" variety. As a precaution, you might make up a list of worst scenarios, present them to your agent, and ask what benefits you would receive, based on your present policy coverage.

A COLLECTION OF BUSINESS TIPS

Never Lease a Postage Meter

"Never lease a postage meter," advises the owner of a mail order business. "You're locked into a three-to-four year contract and you end up paying twice what the machine costs. If I were to drop dead tomorrow, my husband could sell the machine to someone else, but if we were leasing it, he'd have to pay for it for the remainder of the leasing contract. Our meter has proven to be a good ($2,000) investment. Our daily average orders run between 100-250, but we've received as many as 5,000 in one month after the run of an ad. Thus, we figure we're eventually going to save in time what we've spent on the machine."

Get Your Mail on the Fast Track

High-speed electronic mail sorters with optical character readers (OCR) are now installed in many large cities, says the U.S. Postal Service. To get your mail "on the fast track," use only CAPITAL LETTERS, don't punctuate, and use zip codes and two-letter state abbreviations.

Colored envelopes can be a problem, so before ordering them, have the USPS test them for OCR readability. Don't forget that, to be processed electronically, envelopes must meet certain size requirements as well.

Editor's note: The post office may prefer addresses typed in all caps, and it may be easier to computerize names on this basis, but I'll continue to use upper and lower case when typing addresses because it creates a more personal look to my mailings—something that's as important to my business as speed of delivery.

Are You Wasting Postage?

Pitney Bowes, maker of postal meters and scales, says: "If you don't have an electronic mailing scale, you're probably paying more postage than you have to. If the weight indicator of a mechanical scale is on the line between one postage price and another, most people go with the higher amount to be safe. This can mean paying as much as 30 percent in extra postage."

TRAF The Paper on Your Desk

In her book, *The Organized Executive* (W. W. Norton & Co.), Stephanie Winston suggests that you TRAF all the paper on your desk. TRAF is an acronym for the four things you can do with any piece of paper, she says. You can *Toss* it (in the wastebasket), *Refer* it, *Act* on it, or *File* it.

Have They Got Your Number?

If you're receiving aggravating pre-recorded messages from businesses organizations who are trying to sell you something, you can get your name removed from such national calling lists. Just make this request to: The Direct Marketing Association. (Address is in the Resource Chapter.)

Beware of Pyramid Schemes!

Riding the entrepreneurial wave of the 80s is a new bunch of pyramid schemes taking gullible investors for millions of dollars. There's a world of difference between legitimate multi-level sales companies and the unlawful schemes that promise instant wealth.

If you're tempted by a new offer, first send for the free pamphlet, "Pyramid Schemes—Not What They Seem," from the Direct Selling Education Foundation. (Address in resource chapter.)

Warning About Barter Clubs

An *NHBR* reader was encouraged by a friend to pay a $50 membership fee to consign $300 worth of her products to the barter showroom. Although her items were quickly snatched up, there was little or nothing of interest to her, she reported. "In the last two years, I have been able to get an electronic bug zapper at a greatly inflated price, and $50 off a printing bill. I've made dozens of phone calls to the barter system trying to get something I could use. Someone must be getting something out of all this," she concludes, "but it sure hasn't worked for me. What I got, mainly, was a $350 lesson."

Employer's Identification Number

If you change your business name, do you need to get a new employer's identification number? No, says IRS. A letter in the editor's file reads: "You should have only one employer identification number, even if you operate more than one business. This is also true if you are an individual owner or a partnership. You should keep this number and continue to use it even if you relocate your business in a different part of the country."

Help From Sheltered Workshops

"If you have a lot of tedious work to be done—like stuffing thousands of catalogs into envelopes—be sure to check out your local sheltered workshop," a reader advises. "They saved me hundreds of dollars. Everyone worries about quality, but how can you mess up on a job like that? Either you get the catalog in the envelope and seal it, or you don't. I was very pleased with the work they did for me."

Editor's Note: Through the years, several readers have told me they've been more than satisfied with the work done by such organizations. Routine work of any kind—from hand-painting to packaging, stuffing, cutting, etc. can be done at reasonable prices. In addition, you may avoid problems with the Labor Department or IRS, who might consider other workers you hire as employees, instead of independent contractors.

Help for Aging Eyes

As we age, our vision changes, and it gets harder to see the fine print. Before you invest in a pair of prescription lenses, try out the inexpensive magnifying glasses readily available in drug stores and other places where sunglasses are sold. If your vision is good for distance, a $10 pair of magnifying glasses may solve your problem when it comes to reading fine print or doing detail work.

After this note appeared in *NHBR,* a reader responded: "What a terrific idea! My bifocal glasses are set for distance and arm's length work. Now I use the magnifying glasses at the sewing machine and for needlework I've got to be close to."

Editor's note: I recently saw clip-on magnifying glasses in a Brookstone catalog. (See resource chapter for address.)

It Pays to Ask

When a new business owner decided to take an expensive business course, she requested a discount because of the small nature of her business. "Within a few days, a representative called to tell me I could pay $100 instead of $150," she wrote. "It certainly pays to ask!"

Check and DOUBLE-CHECK It!

After a reader gave her catalog artwork to a professional, who "cleaned it up" for her, she discovered, only after it was printed, that they had made some picture changes she hadn't noticed earlier. Later, when they did a flyer for her, she printed and mailed 2500 copies only to discover they had omitted her address. Now, she says, "I think it's a good idea to check material ten times or more and, if possible, keep it on your bulletin board for a week to make sure everything's okay before it's printed."

Editor's Note: Good advice. Remember that when you write your own copy, your eyes often end up seeing what your brain remembers, not what's actually there. For this reason, it is incredibly difficult to proofread your own material and find all the mistakes or omissions.

Federal Information Centers

Federal Information Centers (FICs) serve as a central point of contact for people with questions about the Federal Government and its services. If you have not been able to find an answer to one of your questions, the FIC will either answer it or refer you to a government office that can.

See the resource chapter to order a brochure on how to reach your nearest FIC.

NEWEST CATCH PHRASE in the home of a periodical publisher still learning about bulk mailings and the inner workings of the postal system:

"Your rubber bands are all wrong!"

QUOTE OF THE MONTH:

"If it weren't for the last minute, nothing would get done."

CHARACTER TRAITS THAT
SPELL S-U-C-C-E-S-S IN BUSINESS

By Jan A. DeYoung

In my experience counseling with countless small businesses, many of them homebased, I have found some special traits characteristic of those that have been most successful. I would like to share some of these insights with you.

Those individuals who were successful tended to possess a cluster of attributes. They were persistent. They based their decisions on factual information. They minimized risk. They learned by doing and getting involved with everything in the business.

They made a conscious and total commitment to the needs of the business. They worked harder and longer and were not discouraged by the endless daily problems they faced.

They clearly understood what business they were in and they set boundaries on their activities that were not too broad as to fragment their energy, but not so narrow as to exclude opportunities.

Service was a primary goal. There was a conscious effort to provide support to other people and this became the reward for their activities more so than the profit they made.

They started the business with a minimum amount of capital which forced them to be more attentive to their market, more aware of their costs, and more innovative in solving problems they faced. In the initial stages, it allowed them to survive in a smaller economic niche because they had lower overhead commitments.

Those that started the business with a new idea worked the idea out entirely, examining all its ramifications, and kept developing it until they were certain of its validity before they started the business.

They adopted the rational strategy of going slow in both starting and operating their business. This allowed them opportunity to correct errors before those errors were irreparable. When starting the business it allowed time to observe feedback, to do those things they had not planned on, and to build a larger community for the support of their business. As the businesses became established, making small incremental changes allowed time to see the results of each change.

All businesses had at a minimum a rudimentary set of records which provided a reflection or barometer on the health of the business.

They were aware of the community or environment in which their business existed, including their suppliers, employees, customers, friends, and relatives. These groups became the most important asset of the business as they were looked to for advice, financing, new customers, etc.

They paid their bills promptly, indicating their understanding of each business' role in the chain of interdependency that affects all businesses. When temporary financial problems were encountered, it was important to have the respect and support of the businesses that supplied it.

Finally, there was a recognition of the endless opportunities for having fun in their businesses. The people enjoyed what they were doing and it was natural to have fun where friends and relatives participated and where all understood the role they served. Building fun into their business brought vitality to much of the daily task. "Fun" was not something that was relegated to be bought after work with money they had earned.

This is an excerpt from a taped address given by Jan A. DeYoung, Training & Publications Manager, Small Business Development Center, Iowa State University, Ames, Iowa.

Working Smarter—With the Help of a Computer

At this time, most homebased businesses are not computerized. One reason, I believe, is that technology is moving faster than most people. Another is that most homebased businesses are owned by women, who appear to be less receptive to computers than men.

Since my audience is largely women, I've decided it is a worthy goal to encourage and motivate women to become computer literate and consider the many ways this remarkable machine can improve both their personal and home business lives.

When I wrote the computer chapter for *Homemade Money*, I did not have a computer, but I *was* computer literate and knew exactly what I wanted a computer to do for my own business. That's the first and most important step you can take if you're still in the dreaming stage where a computer is concerned.

Some 40 men and women in my home business network contributed to the new computer chapter in the revised and expanded 1987 edition of *Homemade Money*. They shared insight gained from experience with their individual computer systems, and outlined the many ways a computer was helping them. They talked about their curious love/hate relationship with their equipment, explained how and why computers save time, and how use of this saved time can lead to increased profits.

It's important to emphasize that a computer will not save the kind of time that affords you more leisure; rather, it enables you to do more for your business. Like capital that is often plowed back into a growing business, time saved by computer technology is similarly used. A couple of months after I had been using my computer on a daily basis, I reflected on the volume of work I had accomplished on one particular day, suddenly realizing that the same amount of work would have taken me at least three days to do without the computer. No matter how you carve it, that's progress. I'm working a lot smarter these days, to be sure.

Even more important than increased profitability and greater efficiency in a business, perhaps, is the surprising impact a computer tends to make on one's personal life.

For instance, many of my book's contributors pointed to a discovery of creativity or organizational abilities they didn't realize they had. Others explained how conquering their computer gave them new confidence in their abilities and automatically led them into exciting businesses. Individuals once hampered by the demands of a typewriter suddenly found themselves able to write, design, and brainstorm on a computer.

My research to date indicates that an individual's initial fear of computer technology is seldom justified. With time and patience, *and the desire to do so*, anyone can master a computer and learn to use it productively in both their homebased business and personal lives.

As author Elyse Sommer confirms: "The computer cured me of a lifetime sense of inadequacy *vis-a-vie* machines and anything too mathematical. It took only the initial leap of faith to make me realize that a computer is only as smart as what I put into it. And it took only a smidgeon longer to realize that you tame your computer with logic and not math skills. Naturally, fine-tuning your logical skills to solve computer problems carries over to everything else you do in life."

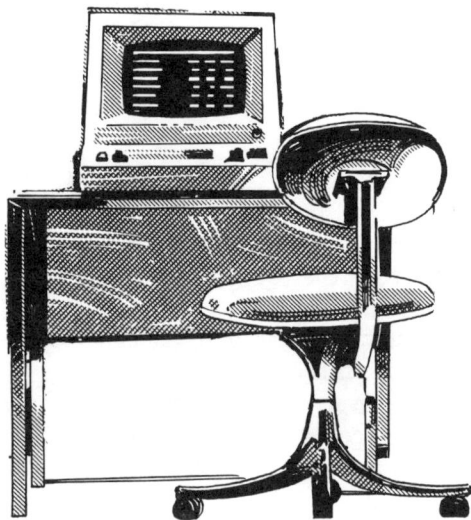

Moneytalk

4.

This chapter is all about money — how to manage it, save it, invest it, collect it, borrow it, and keep as much of it in your bank account as possible.

Several financial experts have contributed articles to *NHBR* in the past, and I'm grateful to them for letting me reprint their information in this book. I know it will benefit you greatly.

Since I'm no financial expert, I don't have a lot to say on this topic, but I do want to tell you about a couple of my "money experiences" and pass on a collection of reader tips on how to collect bounced checks and avoid bad checks as well.

Who Says Banks Don't Make Mistakes?

The next time your bank statement doesn't balance, don't automatically assume the error is yours. Banks make mistakes, too, I learned. One month, while balancing my checkbook, I discovered that the bank showed a balance for my account of $1,000 less than it should have been. My heart practically stopped! I then spent the next hour in a cold sweat looking for the error. Found it, too.

I had written a check to the postmaster for $237...and the bank had taken one THOUSAND two-hundred thirty-seven dollars from my account. If I hadn't been building up a reserve to pay off my line-of-credit loan, I'd have had checks bouncing from here to kingdom come. When I brought this to the bank's attention, the head bookkeeper said, "Oh, an encoding error. We'll put the thousand in your account at once, and double-check our records at the same time."

"Does this kind of thing happen often?" I asked, in total amazement.

"Encoding errors are common," she replied calmly.

"And what would you have done if all my checks had started to bounce, and my creditors ended up being charged for those bounced checks?" I persisted.

"We would have taken care of it," she said. Somehow I got the feeling they do this often.

Lesson learned? I used to put off balancing my checkbook because I'm always so careful when I enter figures. Now I check the statements as soon as they come in.

Collecting a Bounced Check

I'm extremely fortunate to have the kind of business in which bad checks are rare. My customers are, by and large, among the most honest people in the country, I'm sure. In the past six years, we have had only two or three bounced checks a year, and in most cases, individuals made good on them. Sometimes a person moves and closes out a checking account too early; generally, however, the reason for a bad check is "insufficient funds" — which can happen to anyone for a number of reasons.

Some banks automatically put checks through a second time, and there is usually a fee if the check bounces. If it does bounce on the second pass through, and your letters to the check-writer fail to get action, you have another option.

Take the check to your bank and ask them to collect for you. There is a fee for this (around $5), payable only if collection is completed. Your bank will instruct the bank on which the check is drawn to hold it (usually for ten days), and as soon as funds are deposited in the account, they put the check through for you. (Note: The ten-day cycle can be repeated more than once.)

A reader who receives thousands of checks annually from her mail order customers told me she asked her bank not to send her NSF (non-sufficient funds) checks until after sending them through a second time.

"I am not charged a penalty for depositing bad checks (except Canadian)," she said, "and I lose nothing by having the bank automatically put them through a second time. Since I began doing this, the number of checks that bounce twice is minuscule. While I used to have 8-10 bad checks per month, I now might have two or three at most. I think what happened was, I was so slow getting them in that they were out of money again by the time the check came through a second time." She concludes: "I have found small NSF checks are not worth the 22-cent stamp it takes to go after them. People just won't make good on them."

Another reader suggested this tactic for twice-bounced checks: "Notify the customer and ask for a money order to cover the funds by a definite date. If no response, write a second time. This time, inform your customer that if funds are not received by a second deadline, you will have no other alternative but to report his name to your local Check-Guarantee Company, as well as the Credit Bureau in your customer's area. (Note: Check-guarantee companies may not accept checks from non-members, but your customer may not know this. Also, the fear of being reported to the credit bureau may coerce them to action.)

"Be authoritative!" she concludes. "Let them know you mean business."

This kind of scare tactic doesn't always work, of course. When I tried something similar on a customer whose check was written on a closed account, she ignored my first two letters. My third letter, sent two months after the check bounced, threatened to report her as a bad check-writer. Now *that* letter got an immediate response. No money, of course; just a lot of insults. My "bad customer" told me I had the literary skills of a fourth grader, and was obviously the meanest woman in Illinois. She was going to tell the world about me, too! I just threw the whole mess in the wastebasket. I don't need money from people like this. (And, just for the record, I'm NOT the meanest woman in Illinois.)

Collection Idea

"This collection technique has worked twice for me, and may work for others," a reader reports.

"After three notices and several phone calls to an establishment that is overdue (usually 90 days by that time), I send a certified letter, restricted delivery, to the owner. There is a modest charge for this, but you get back a receipt which has the owner's signature. The letter states my intention of turning the matter over to my attorney if the bill is not paid within three days of receipt of the letter.

"The post office will attempt to deliver this mail several times and, in fact, has two weeks to try before it is returned to you with the dates listed of attempted delivery."

Avoiding Bad Checks in the First Place

"The best way to collect a bad check is to avoid it in the first place," one reader told me, adding, " Always observe and *feel* a transaction as it is being made. That uncomfortable sale will most likely be the one that results in a bad check. (A teller can nearly always remember the transaction that causes her to be out-of-balance.) In those situations where you feel uncomfortable, ask more questions of the customer and get complete information. In addition to identification, obtain the individual's place of employment and phone. Not currently employed? Beware. Be aware!"

These tips are fine if you happen to collect money from people face to face. But what about mail order sellers?

"Note the check number on all payments," one mailer order dealer advises. "This will tell how stable the person is, and how long he or she has banked at one location."

That might help, but it isn't a guarantee. One publisher told me, "Check numbers do not always tell how stable a person is. We received a check number 10796, and it bounced. We've also received may checks numbered between 6-100 that have been good. Interesting to note as well that we received a check for 40 cents that bounced. Wonder how Small Claims Court would handle this?"

You may think it impossible for a 40-cent check to bounce, but I've had at least two 50-cent checks bounce myself. Not impossible, but certainly amazing.

A bank teller in my readership gave me this tip to pass on to readers. In some states, it is a law that checks must carry special code numbers on them, immediately after an individual's imprinted name and address. For example 176 would mean January, 1976; 485 would mean April 1985. "Although this won't tell you if a person knows how to handle an account, it at least gives some idea of how long a person has been established with a bank," says the bank teller.

"I would never accept a check without a name imprint," says one business owner, "without waiting for it to clear before I delivered the goods. However, any local check can be verified by calling the bookkeeping department of the bank and asking if funds in the account will cover the amount of the check."

If you don't mind a long-distance call, you can get the same information on out-of-state checks. We've done this on occasion with large checks that have made us uncomfortable. Curiously, they've always been good. The ones that bounce are usually for small amounts.

Finally, these thoughts from another mail order seller: "Remember that retailers ask for a picture I.D. as well as one or two major credit cards prior to accepting a personal check. So why shouldn't mail order companies have the same privilege? Insist that orders over a certain amount be accompanied by a credit card number *and signature* (sort of like a credit reference). State on your order form that any returned checks will automatically be processed through the credit card company for the amount of the check *plus* a service charge (go for the full amount allowed by law). In my four years of selling, I have never had a credit card invalid in the case when there was a returned check."

Many states have "bad check laws," of course, and retailers often post a copy in an effort to deter bad checks. *(For an idea of the protection such laws afford, see right.)*

Illinois Bad Check Law

"Any person who writes a check dishonored for lack of funds is now civilly liable and can be sued in small claims court or any appropriate court for three times the amount of the check plus the face value of the check. The minimum you may collect is $100, so if you have a $15 check you can sue for $115. The maximum amount in damages you can collect is $500, so if you have a $600 bad check, you can sue for $1,100. You may also sue for costs such as filing and service fees; these costs are awarded at the judge's discretion."

SHOULD YOUR BUSINESS HAVE CHARGE CARD CAPABILITIES?

> Charge it, please, your customer says. . . but it's not as easy as that if you have a homebased business. Even if you can get this capability for your business, how useful will it be? The following letter from Eugene L. Larson was published in *NEBR* in late 1985, and it drew a number of comments from readers. You'll find them immediately following this article, along with Eugene's present feelings about charge cards. - *Editor*

I just received a charge capability for my business from (X) bank. I had several strikes against me at the start of the approval process, and now that I have the capability, I have doubts about how useful it will be.

Initially, my business was selling ship model half hull kits through mail order. Now that I am expanding the business by offering finished models and a unique model-building tool which I developed, I want to participate in occasional craft shows and conferences. I thought it would be a good idea to be able to accept credit cards so the person without cash or a checkbook does not get away.

Although the total time to obtain a charge capability from the date of first application was only about a month, I had to make some significant but tolerable concessions:

(1) The bank was concerned that a home business without public access to a store would make customer return of merchandise difficult. Thus the customer could legally refuse to pay the charge on his bill if the item could not be returned. This could result in the bank being placed in the middle or being stuck with the charge. This problem (although vague) was resolved by explaining that my mailing address (a P.O.Box) and phone are available in all my products. In addition, I have had only one return in the last 18 months.

(2) The bank does not want mail order charges due to the risks involved in false account numbers. My mail order business has done well based upon check and money order payments. I told the bank that the only charges I would accept would be in person, with the charge card imprinted on the sales slip, and the customer's signature obtained. I figured that I need the charge capability for shows and conferences where I would have the personal contact with the customer.

In negotiating the above items, I was told somewhere along the way that it probably would be easier if I applied to the Bank of (Y) as they have more lenient rules for home businesses. That would mean changing my business account to a bank 15 miles away. And for some reason, my current business account does not have a service charge.

With the above concessions, the bank approved my application following a personal credit check (I assume, since they asked for that type of basic information). However, during the application process I requested literature on the way charge accounts are handled by the bank and what requirements would be placed upon my business. I was told that all this information would be made available if the application were approved.

When I met with the bank official to obtain my package of information, charge slips, imprinter, etc., I discovered the major problem ahead of me. The bank requires that all charges over $50 be authorized by a phone call using either a touch tone phone with all coded information, or verbally to a credit representative. All my products are over $50, with some as high as $350. I now have several options when I'm at a craft show:

(1) Ask a customer to wait while I go to the pay phone (if there is one);

(2) Ask a customer to come back in 30 minutes, hoping that I will have time to make the call (and maybe miss another sale);

(3) Accept the charge immediately and later call for authorization, taking a chance that it may be disapproved, and then I am stuck. Authorizations are based not only upon whether a card is valid, and not stolen, for example, but also upon the credit limit the customer has. If a charge over $50 goes over the credit limit, it will not be approved when the authorization call is made.

The bank established their service charge at a percentage of the total charge (3%), which seemed fair to me. That is subject to review in three months; I guess, based upon my record of sales, errors, bad charges, etc.

Luckily, I guess, all that it has cost me to obtain the charge capability is the time and the one-time $26 charge for the card imprinting machine. However, I am not sure that I will be able to use it.

1987 Update From Eugene

I sent the above article just after receiving credit card capability. Since then, about 18 months, I have processed ONE credit charge from a sale at a national conference. All other sales have been by cash or check. This may be unique to the type of people I deal with, and the fact that I do not attend many conferences and shows. The conferences are attended by avid model builders; they will buy anything associated with building a better model or doing it easier, and I always sell out of my wood thickness sander machines there.

My half hull models (kits and finished) do not sell there. They also do not sell at craft shows, probably because of the price, which is $65 for a kit and over $300 for a finished mode. Most items at a craft show are priced below $20. I find that my sales are much higher through magazine advertising and word-of-mouth.

I must add, though, that I could have had more charges if the bank allowed me to take orders over the phone. I have to tell people that this is not possible, and a check or money order is acceptable. I do not believe this has resulted in one lost sale, but sometimes it is difficult to explain the bank policy on requiring a card imprint and signature on the charge slip.

Last year I processed nearly one thousand checks for my brochure, models, and sander (from $1 to $350 each) and not one was returned for any reason.

The bottom line for me is that I do not believe having the charge capability is such a great advantage.

Ship design at left was adapted from Eugene's business letterhead.

Eugene is a professional and master model builder, Captain of the Washington Ship Model Society, member of and advisor to the Nautical Research Guild, and member of the Northern Virginia Carvers.

He has published several articles in international model magazines, including an article on wood processing and characteristics in the May/June '87 issue of Ships in Scale.

He reports that his new full color brochure has "really boosted sales." Interested readers may order it for $1. (See Eugene's address in the resource chapter.)

The following reader feedback to Eugene's article is typical of the kind of response I usually receive to a timely home-business topic after it's been introduced in *NHBR*. Individuals who are still debating the value of a subscription should remember that each new issue is built on what has gone before. This is what makes *NHBR* a true "networking publication." *No other periodical in the home-business industry consistently draws my kind of reader response.* Don't deny yourself access to this unique business network.

After reading Eugene's article, one reader reported that she had no trouble with her bank, but what proved to be a nightmare was trying to use the large, store-size imprinter (the only one the bank could provide), which required imprinting of the dollar amount of sales. "In the confusion of using the machine for the first time, on an aluminum folding table not cut out for such equipment, I ruined the first charge slip, and accidentally imprinted an outrageous amount of $11,015.73 on another slip. Now that lady is not going to be happy about this," she wrote.

In this case, the bank advised it was okay to cross out the incorrect amount and write in the proper total. As for costs of this service, this reader said she paid a one-time charge of $17, plus $55 for the imprinter. The bank charges 5% on amounts charged, but no service charge if the account happens to be dormant a few months.

Another reader reported that her bank charges her account $5/month when no slips are processed (something that would certainly prompt Eugene Larson to drop his charge privilege, and yet another point to remember if you're thinking about getting charge card privileges). This reader added, "I was told that the availability of a charge service would increase my sales by a third, but one year later, I find I have processed a total of FIVE charge slips. Since I only use the machine at craft shows from October to December, I've decided it isn't worth the cost to me."

The owner of a thriving cottage industry writes, "Our bank has been super about all our arrangements (but then I deal with a very knowledgeable woman banker). We use Visa and MasterCard for our mail order business, and I had no trouble getting it from the bank. We had about $4,000 in charge sales in the past two months, and not one bad credit card. We approve (by toll-free number) each charge sale, but have never had a charge turned down. Since we have to have an address to ship to, this may be why we have had no trouble with the cards. I think this has really helped our sales. We advertise nationally, and I think people find this more comfortable than spending a check. About one-third to one-half of our business has been credit card sales, and people even call to order over the phone with the card."

Why It's Difficult to Get Bank Card Services

This whole topic was originally prompted by a letter from a reader who said she was amazed to learn that the Bank of America did not offer credit cards to customers who work out of their homes. "They deal only with businesses in some sort of public place," she reported. "They obviously have no idea what's taking place in homes today. The regional bank office called to confirm

Checks Marked "Payment in Full"

If a customer pays less than the amount he's billed, and sends a check marked "Payment in Full," can you deposit that check without prejudicing the right to recover the balance?

Yes, says The Book of Inside Information (Boardroom Books), but only if there is no dispute as to the amount actually owed. But it is suggested that you stamp the check with a statement, "Check is accepted without prejudice and with full reservation of all rights under Section 1-207 of the Uniform Commercial Code."

If there is a dispute as to the amount owed, it's best to reject the check and demand full payment. Otherwise, you run the risk that payment already made will be deemed to have settled the disputed claim for the lesser amount.

that the RULES are NO mail order or phone order businesses will be given bankcard privileges."

Writes a teacher who has found charge privileges an invaluable asset in her crafts business: "After telling my students about it, one of them tried to get a card and was turned down by several banks here because she was a home business. They were willing to give her a commercial account, but not the charge card privileges. They told her that home business people had not been reliable in the past, and had taken the money from the accounts before the charge card firms had verified the charges. The banks were then losing losing money when charges were not valid."

As this teacher pointed out, the percentage of bad charges are likely to be much higher from retail outlets, due to sheer volume of sales, and this sounds like just another excuse not to deal with home business people.

There are, however some legitimate reasons why banks may not want to approve bank card services these days. As you're no doubt aware, there is a lot of fraud in the credit card industry, and many banks are simply refusing to accept new applications from anyone without a prior banking history.

And those who do have bank card privileges are finding that banks often make chargebacks for as many as 65 different reasons— all without the merchant's permission. (I picked up on this information in a •trade paper for the direct mail industry.) If a transaction turns out to be fraudulent, a bank can zap a merchant's account for up to a year after the sale was made. (This fact is confirmed by Dottie Walters' remarks below.)

In suspicious instances, to protect against the use of stolen credit card numbers, you can ask for the name of the issuing bank, something a thief won't know. Then you can call that bank to verify the customer's name and address.

Special Tips from Dottie Walters

Dottie Walters, who publishes *Sharing Ideas Newsmagazine*, originally published the following tips in her own newsletter, then gave me permission to pass them along to my readers:

Even though you get phone clearance on the card, the card companies can come back within 12 months and do either of the following:

(1) Charge the entire amount back to your bank account without notice, leaving your bank to bounce your checks;

(2) Tell you that you must send in new charges from your customers in the amount of a declined charge. When YOU have paid that declined customer's bill in full, the credit card company will then allow you to send in new orders and be paid for them.

This is particularly difficult with customers and clients outside the U.S. GOOD IDEA: Suggest that your out-of-U.S. client who wants to use a credit card go to the bank and get a cashier's check against his credit card, and to send you the check. This still allows the client to make small payments, but prevents your being stuck up to twelve months later.

$ $ $ $ $ $ $ $ $ $ $ $

Which Bills To Pay First?

When your money just won't stretch far enough, certain bills should be paid first to keep your credit history clean.

Banks, finance companies and major credit card companies (Visa, MasterCard, Sears, etc.) generally report to credit agencies right away, so pay them first.

Gas company credit charges and American Express may not report late payments until an account is several months overdue. The same is true of doctor and dentist bills, utilities, rent or mortgage payments, according to an article in McCall's.

If you can't make a business loan payment, or the full mortgage payment, ask the bank if you can just pay the interest for the one month. You may be surprised at how understanding a bank can be in this situation.

$ $ $ $ $ $ $ $ $ $ $ $

Dottie adds, "When a bank turned down one of our speakers, she called for advice. I suggested she go to another bank, give her home address, but not *say* it was home. Just be quiet," I told her. "It went right through. (If there is an apartment number, call it a 'Suite Number'.)"

Apparently a lot of home business owners have caught on to this little trick. I'm seeing a growing number of suite numbers in letters asking for my brochure. What's amusing to me is that people are using them on letters scribbled on yellow note paper. I wonder who they think they're fooling? Also a dead giveaway are addresses with "Court", "Lane," and other residential-sounding street names. Before long this trick will be overdone to the point of silliness and many home business owners will be back where they started from, looking for other new ways to make people think they're anything but homebased. My advice is to work on your business image, making it as professional as possible. Then you won't have to make excuses about being homebased. High quality business products and services speak for themselves.

A Line of Credit

In my experience, banks do not discriminate against homebased business owners, so long as they have legitimate, profitable businesses and can deliver the kind of kind of financial reports they want to see.

When I started shopping for a line of credit after 4 years in business, I visited two local banks, explaining my needs and presenting each of them with what I felt was an impressive package of business and financial information. Both banks indicated their interest in loaning money, but at the first bank, I spoke with one of the regular bank officers; at the second, I met with the bank's vice president. I figured if I was going to "get friendly" with a bank, I ought to be dealing with as high an official as possible. (I'd always heard it said that you deal not with banks, but with bankers.)

When the banker asked what collateral I was offering, I said with a smile, "You're looking at it: me. I believe the information in my portfolio will convince you this is enough."

He, in turn, pointed out (with a smile) that the bank's depositors aren't too thrilled with this kind of collateral, and said that if I were truly serious about building my business, I ought to be willing to risk a second mortgage on the house, or give up access to the family savings account.

"No," I said. "It's a matter of principle at this point. I'm tired of having to use personal funds to advance my business. I've proven myself, shown what I could do with an initial investment of just $1,000 — and besides, I have it on good authority that business loans do not *have* to be secured in this way, particularly when one's credit is excellent."

Grinning, he took another look at my papers. In the end, my ploy worked. I walked out of the bank with an unsecured line of credit (signature only) for $10,000 — more than enough to meet my needs at any given time. All it took to get it was the right paperwork and a little moxie.

Shopping For the Right Bank

While I'm talking about banks, let me remind you that all banks do not charge the same amount for handling specific transactions. In fact, if you were to pick six banks at random and ask each of them the questions indicated at right, you'd be amazed at how much you might save each month by placing your account in a particular bank or savings and loan association.

In Jane Bryant Quinn's "Money Facts" column in *Woman's Day*, she once noted that some financial institutions levy heavy fees on small depositors in hopes they will take their business elsewhere. She added that smaller banks and S&Ls generally charge less than large ones.

In the past, savings and loan associations were where people put their savings; they kept checking accounts in banks. These days, S&L Associations are calling themselves "savings *banks*" and offering their customers "checking privileges," often without any charge at all. Mail order sellers like myself would go broke with a regular checking account in a bank because charges are made for all the things mentioned above. But there is one drawback in having your business account with a savings and loan association.

While an S&L will be happy to finance your house, car and other personal purchases, you may not be able to get a business loan. And, when you have to open a second business checking account in another bank just to get a business loan or line of credit, you immediately run into cash flow problems. Keeping your money in two places can get tricky when cash is at a premium.

A friend of mine who managed to secure three separate lines of credit had to open the usual business accounts to get them. She spent a lot of time transferring money from one checking account to another to cover paybacks on the loans and in time had to give up some of the credit because there just wasn't enough money to go around.

Too little money in an account will have a lot to do with the rate of interest you'll pay when you take a business loan. A practically-empty checking account means you'll probably pay several points over prime to get a loan; whereas (my banker just told me), if you had in your checking account about the same amount you wanted to borrow, you would, in effect, be financing your own loan, and you'd be likely to get a lower interest rate accordingly.

Also, when you decide to ask for a business loan, remember that banks think bigger than you do. You may only need a thousand dollars, but my bank, for instance, won't give a business loan for anything less than $2500. The general advice seems to be to always ask for more than you need. If you get it, you can always put it in a savings account for a month, let it draw interest to offset what you're paying for this money, then pay back what you don't need the next month. This will only help to further establish your credit with the lending bank.

Moneysaving
Questions to Ask a Bank

1. Is there a charge for each deposit made?

2. Is there a charge for each out-of-state check deposited?

3. Is there a charge for each check written, or a fee for checks ordered by the hundred?

4. Is there a penalty if your balance falls below a certain point?

5. Is interest paid on the checking account balance?

6. Does the bank or S&L offer a line of credit to established businesses?

7. Are bank card charge services available, in the event you wish to offer this to your customers?

By Richard L. Duffy

HOW TO BORROW MONEY WITHOUT GOING BONKERS

It is unlikely that a bank would lend a beginning businessperson thousands, or even hundreds, of dollars without a good business plan and some form of collateral to offer as security for the loan. But here's a creative suggestion for borrowing $10,000 that might work for you.

Suppose you need $10,000 and you know the bank won't lend it to you based on your current financial condition. Since you want to stay in control of your business, you prefer not to take in a partner who would invest in the business, because you'd have to share whatever profits are earned. You are hesitant to ask friends or relatives to write you a check for $10,000 on the promise that you'll pay them back, since you feel the relationship will get testy if your repayment drags on longer than anticipated. But, you *do* know someone with the $10,000 and the capacity and willingness to lend you the money. We'll call that "someone" Susan Jones.

Suggest to Susan that you wish to obtain a bank loan "hypothecated" by her $10,000. You would ask Susan to withdraw $10,000 from her existing savings account and open a *new* savings account of exactly $10,000 at the financial institution where you want to borrow. Susan then pledges her new savings passbook to the bank as security for your loan by hypothecating it to the bank. She turns it over to the lender and signs a "Hypothecation Agreement" that gives the lender control over her passbook during the time your loan remains unpaid.

In turn, you borrow the $10,000 from the bank in your business name and pay off the loan, including interest, in accordance with a payment schedule you have established with the bank.

What are the benefits from this type of borrowing arrangement? First, Susan does not own a piece of your business, or your profits. Second, she can still "see" the $10,000, which remains in her name, since she keeps earning interest on her deposited funds and the bank sends her periodic statements of this interest. Further, she may, at any time, withdraw any part of the funds remaining over your unpaid loan balance. Third, you are establishing a payment track record, or credit history, with the lender, and can use this loan as a credit reference. Fourth, Susan will feel more confident about your repayment of the loan because you will be dealing directly with the bank and she will be counting on the bank to collect the money from you.

Obviously, this method of borrowing requires finding someone with an available asset of $10,000 or more in value; an asset which, incidentally, could also be in the form of stocks, bonds, or notes receivable. When achieved, it combines you, the bank, and your benefactor in a businesslike manner while providing you with a benefactor's capital and a bank's credit during the period your business is getting started.

Preparation: The Key to Success

Rich Duffy, a banker for over twenty years and now a financial consultant, is frequently called upon to put together loan packages for new businesses. He has sat on both sides of the loan officer's desk and knows from experience how uncomfortable, or frustrated, the ordinary homebased or small businessperson feels when he needs to borrow money from a bank.

"Judge where you stand *before* you approach your banker, Rich cautions, "and be ready to answer the questions that are important to you both. Preparation is the key to success in getting a bank loan."

THE KEY TO FINANCIAL CONTROL

by Gerry Dodd & Ann Blair

"How can I deal with cash shortages? How can I be more certain about my plans for expansion? Why can't my banker seem to understand the tremendous potential of my business?"

These are but a few of the many questions common to small business folk around the country which can be answered with a simple management technique: *CASH FLOW PROJECTION AND ANALYSIS*. This article explains the importance and application of this technique.

Cash shortages are a major problem for most self-employed people and small business owners who have painfully inadequate cash reserves to deal with the inevitable slumps in business activity. Two rules apply to the flow of cash:

(1) The cash coming in from sales must eventually equal or exceed the cash going out;

(2) There must be enough cash available for bills as they are due.

The impact of cash crises can be lessened through planning. Adept managers carefully monitor their monthly cash position. Solid financial data is a basis for making tighter projections.

A CASH FLOW PROJECTION is a monthly budget showing how much cash is needed, when it is needed and where it will come from. It focuses your attention on the "bottom line" — your expected cash position when all is said and done. It compares receipts or cash coming in against expenditures.

Ideally, a cash flow projection is for a full 12-month period. It's done in pencil so that it can be changed. While you familiarize yourself with the process, forecast for shorter periods (*e.g.*, three months) but gradually build up to six months and then a year.

Columns are provided for "projected" and for posting "real" figures at the end of each month. The "projected" cash flow is an estimate of monthly income and expenses. Use whatever records you have to construct it.

If you are just starting in business, the process will be more difficult since there is little on which to base calculations. You may feel that you're reaching into thin air for figures, but these "guesstimates" will provide benchmarks for measuring your progress towards certain goals. Anything you do to plan is better than a shot in the dark!

As a rule, project lower-than-hoped-for income, and higher-than-expected expenses. Certain assumptions about costs and your ability to reach the market will be made (be sure to record them in a notebook for future

CASH FLOW — JOE'S SALES & SERVICE

1985 MONTH OF:	AUGUST Proj.	AUGUST Real	SEPTEMBER Proj.	SEPTEMBER Real	OCTOBER Proj.	OCTOBER Real	(through July 1986) Proj.	Real	Proj.	Real
CASH ON HAND	2,235	2,235	1,005	1,820	55					
RECEIPTS — RETAIL SALES	1,900	2,255	2,280		2,740					
SERVICE WORK	625	560	750		900					
COLLECTIONS	150	175	200		150					
TOTAL CASH AVAILABLE	4,910	5,225	4,235		3,845					
EXPENDITURES — MERCHANDISE	750	834	1,000		1,000					
OWNER'S DRAWING	1,000	800	1,000		1,000					
PROFESSIONAL SERV.	75	50	100		—					
TRUCK EXPENSE	350	380	350		350					
REPAIRS + MAIN.	75	54	75		75					
BIZ. SUPPLIES	150	129	150		150					
POSTAGE	200	75	200		200					
ADVERTISING	400	300	600		500					
RENT	200	200	200		200					
UTILITIES	40	37	40		60					
TELEPHONE	70	89	80		80					
EQUIPMENT	145	145	145		145					
MISCELLANEOUS	350	312	350		350					
TOTAL EXPENDITURES	3,905	3,405	4,290		4,110					
ENDING POSITION	1,005	1820	55		(265)					
ACCOUNTS PAYABLE (end of month)	+155									

Sample cash flow report, courtesy of the authors.

reference). You'll need to develop a sales plan or marketing strategy and estimate your rate of growth in each area of activity. You must generate enough sales to pay your expenses.

With a three-month projection in hand, it's time to compare what really happens against what was expected. Close your books at the end of the first month and fill in the "real" column on your cash flow. Do this opportunely; *i.e.*, within the first five business days of the new months. Tally income and subtract expenses to find your cash position. Then, fill in "accounts payable" at the bottom of the page (an important step—if you haven't paid your bills, things will look better than they are).

Now analyze what happened. Look for the big discrepancies between your real and projected figures. Did your plans work out as expected? If not, why not, and what does this mean for the future?

Don't be upset if your initial projections are way off! It will take about three months to gain basic forecasting skills. With time, you'll learn to predict (and, therefore, plan for) the peaks and slumps in your business cycle, and the value of the cash flow process will become more clear. Decide now to give it at least a three-month trial.

You are now "looking at the bottom line" so that more educated decisions about the future of your business can be made. If something isn't working as expected, you'll want to know why, and you'll want to adjust your plans and strategies accordingly. Sudden growth, seasonal fluctuations, population shifts, changes in competition and mounting receivables can all affect the flow of cash.

A Study of Cash Flow Figures Can Help You:

- Look at your business more objectively
- Get a better idea of its growth and potential
- Target customers and services which provide a higher margin of profit and stability
- Forecast a serious business slump in time to line up a bank loan
- Deal more effectively with a banker
- See where you have to cut costs
- Budget for special expenditures
- Determine when and at what rate to expand your business

As you study the differences between your real and projected figures, ask such questions as:

- Why are sales up? Down?

- Why are certain products/services selling better than others?

- What am I going to do next month to keep sales up, to improve sales or better promote best-selling items?

- What new products/services could I add in six months to complement my present line?

- Why did certain expenses go up? Down?

- Can I cut back on some expenses and still keep sales up?

- Should I shop around for different suppliers with better prices, quality or services?

- Do I have any major expenses coming due in the next three months for which I have to plan?

Based on this analysis, amend your projections for the following two months and project one additional month so that you are always three months ahead.

At this point, you should know of potential cash shortages in the next three months. If you predict shortages, develop a strategy for dealing with them. Seek a short-term loan, cut down on expenses, offer a discount to customers for paying promptly, etc. Plan ahead to avoid last-minute crisis management!

Gerry and Ann run their own publishing and consulting firm. They provide basic, practical management information to self-employed people and micro-businesses using knowledge gained from running many economic development and small business assistant programs. Their series of five Management Workbooks for Self-Employed People *is listed in the resource chapter.*

TAX TIPS FROM JULIAN BLOCK

How Long to Keep Tax Records

You need no reminder to hold on to your tax records in case your returns are questioned by the Internal Revenue Service. But just how long do you need to save those old records that clutter up your closets and desk drawers? Unfortunately, there is no flat cutoff. The IRS says the answer depends on what's in those records and the type of transaction involved.

While the IRS doesn't even require you to keep copies of your returns, it warns that supporting records must be kept for "as long as their contents may become material in the administration of any Internal Revenue law." In plainer language, hang on to receipts, cancelled checks, and whatever else might help support income, deductions, or other items on your return, at least until the statue of limitations runs out for an IRS audit or for you to file a refund claim, should you find an error after filing.

As a general rule, the IRS has three years from the filing deadline to take a crack at your return. For example, a return for 1987, with a filing deadline of April 15, 1988, remains subject to an audit until April, 1991.

Once the three-year period runs out, it's usually safe to dispose of your receipts and other supporting records. But there are exceptions to the general rule, and they can be significant.

The tax code gives the IRS six years from the filing deadline to begin an examination if you omit from the return an amount that runs to more than 25 percent of the income you reported on it. There is no time limit on when the IRS can begin an audit if you fail to file a return or you file one that is considered fraudulent. The tax for that year can be assessed "at any time."

Copies of Returns

You should retain copies of your old tax returns for at least five years. They are always helpful as a guide for making out future returns.

Copies of your returns can also prove helpful in case the IRS claims you failed to file them. Want to really nail things down at filing time? You can hand deliver a return to your local IRS office, which will stamp the receipt date on both the filed copy and the copy you keep. That way, there should be no question that your return was filed.

If you failed to copy your returns and now need them, get IRS Form 4506, "Request for Copy of Tax Form," from your nearest IRS office, which is listed in the telephone directory. You must file a separate Form 4506 for each return requested. If you have moved, send the form to the IRS service center where the returns were filed, not to the service center for your current address.

The IRS does not keep returns as long as you should. It usually destroys the originals six years after the filing date.

When The Bottom Line Is Not Black

Did your business operate at a loss last year. Then you should know how to take advantage of a special tax break that allows you to use your loss to recover or reduce taxes paid in other years. The key to this opportunity is Internal Revenue Code Section 172, which permits a business that suffers a net operating loss (expenses exceed income) to carry that loss back to earlier years or forward to future years.

One option is to use your net operating loss to first reduce profits in the three previous years, so as to generate a refund of taxes paid on income for those years—an especially useful tactic when cash is tight. What if the loss exceeds three years' income? Then carry forward the unused part of any loss not employed as an income offset and apply it, until used up, against profits in the following 15 years.

Another option available to an ailing business is to skip the entire carryback for any given year and simply carry forward that year's net operating loss, provided it is advantageous to do so. This maneuver might be preferable when, for example, your income was taxed at low rates for the previous three years and you expect to be in higher brackets in future years.

To illustrate how these rules work, assume that the bottom line is not black for 1987 and that 1984, 1985 and 1986 were low-income years. With that scenario, you should do better by electing to forego the carryback, assuming you can use up the net operating loss during the carryforward years that begin in 1986.

The law gives you ample time to assess your tax situation for 1987 and decide whether to make the election. You have until the filing deadline, including extensions, for your 1987 return. Once made, however, the election is irrevocable.

Plan to go the carryback route? Be mindful that the IRS insists on a strict chronological order. Your net operating loss for 1987 must first be carried back and deducted on your return for 1984 and to obtain a refund of part or all of your taxes for 1984. If the loss exceeds your income for 1984, the unused part can then be carried to your return for 1985. If the remaining part exceeds your income for 1985, it can then be carried back to your return for 1986. If there is still a part of the loss for 1987 left, it can then be carried over to your return for 1988, etc.

Filing for a carryback refund does not mean that your return for 1987 will be automatically flagged for examination. Nevertheless, you should be aware that a refund claim might prompt the IRS to not only question your return for 1987, but also to take a look at your returns for earlier years.

It is wise to determine in advance of an audit whether some of the figures on your returns cannot stand a close look. The examination could conceivably uncover errors that erase the hoped-for refund and entitle the IRS to exact back taxes, plus interest. Note also that approval of a refund claim does not bar a later audit.

For detailed information on the often complex carryback/carryforward rules, contact your local IRS office for a free copy of *Net Operating Losses* (Publication 536).

Julian Block covers taxes for Prentice-Hall Information Services in Paramus, New Jersey and is an attorney in Larchmont, New York. He is also the author of Julian Block's Guide to Year-Round Tax Savings. *(See resource chapter).*

Other Tax Tips

● **Putting Personal Property into Business Usage.** What happens when you start a business and begin to use personal property that may already be paid for, or in the process of being paid for?

You *can* depreciate this equipment on either a cost or market value basis, whichever is less, says Bernard Kamoroff, author of *Small-Time Operator*. But how do you determine the fair market value?

"Pick a figure and hope you don't have to prove it," quips Kamoroff, adding that, in his experience, IRS seldom questions any reasonable amount.

To be sure, you need the help of a good accountant if you want to save money on your taxes, and for accurate answers to your many tax/bookkeeping/legal questions, make sure you have the latest edition of *Small-Time Operator* on your bookshelf. It's the most popular book of its kind ever printed.

● **When Credit Cards Are Really Handy.** If you end up cash poor at year's end and have a lot of tax-deductible items still unpaid for, remember that you can charge expenses or tax-deductible items on a credit card and take that deduction in the year in which the charge was made.

This is when those checks the charge card companies offer come in handy. You can send one of them to a supplier, take the deduction, and pay the card company later. If using your charge card, note that IRS considers that payment has been made on the date of the credit card transaction—not when you actually pay it.

The one catch is that you must use a third-party credit card such as MasterCard or Visa. You can't use a card issued by the company who supplies the deductible goods or services (department store purchase on a department store card, for instance.)

Source for this information: *IRS Confidential* booklet, prepared by the editors of *Tax Hotline* Newsletter.

● **Getting Aggressive with Your Accountant.** In one of the tax newsletters I read regularly, the editor advised its readers that the IRS has come down hard on those in the tax preparation industry, telling tax preparers, in so many words, that if they get too aggressive in interpreting tax laws, they'll find all their clients being audited.

How does this affect you? It suggests that you may have to be the aggressive one when it comes to claiming all the tax breaks you're entitled to. One way to know you are on firm ground is to be aware of the many legitimate deductions available to every home-business owner (See *Homemade Money* for a complete list). Another is to subscribe to at least one tax periodical to stay informed of changes in the tax laws. Still another is to have a good tax guide on your reference shelf. One such guide is Julian Block's book, mentioned in the tax article in this chapter.

Finally, don't assume that your tax preparer or accountant knows it all or never makes a mistake. Not all accountants even know what a homebased business is, let alone which deductions are standard. If they handle corporate work only, look for another accountant. You want someone who understands *small* business. Remember, too, that mistakes are often made by tax preparers when they're being rushed by clients trying to meet the April 15 deadline. I have *never* received a tax return from even the best accountant that didn't have something wrong with it that had to be changed at the last minute.

● **Sales Tax Problems Ahead.** Because of new sales tax laws recently passed in several states—including California, Oklahoma, South Dakota, Illinois, Indiana, Michigan, Minnesota, Ohio and Wisconsin—businesses across the country, (and mail order dealers in particular) are learning that they're being held liable for the collection of sales tax in states other than their own, even though they have no legal business presence (nexus) in those states. Companies are supposed to obtain a permit from these states, then include that permit number on all advertising. Still under consideration is a federal law that will require ALL out-of-state companies to collect taxes on behalf of customers' home states where taxes apply.

How states with such laws on the books will police them is unknown. Articles in industry magazines have indicated that many small business owners have adopted a "wait-and-see" attitude in the belief that states are unlikely to have the staff to pursue the few tax dollars they're likely to generate. In fact, a tax examiner in Minnesota was quoted in *DM News* as saying this state was primarily interested in high-ticket items, "certainly not $10 items because it's not worth the trouble."

Naturally, major mail order marketers are challenging these state laws, arguing that what the states are trying to do is force direct marketing firms to do something that is impractical, in addition to interfering with interstate commerce, which they say is unconstitutional. Companies that try to comply with all the different state and local sales tax laws are likely to cave in under the paperwork load and possibly be driven out of business, they maintain.

Read *NHBR* to stay up to date on this topic in future.

Believe It Or Not!

A reader sent a clipping from her local paper on what may be the most unusual home business yet.

STOCKHOLM, Sweden: A woman who stole clothes and sold them must be taxed as a business and may deduct any expenses incurred on her shoplifting forays, a court has rule.

The regional court...ruled that the woman, a 32-year-old unidentified teacher ordered to undergo psychiatric treatment as a kleptomaniac, would have to pay taxes on $55,000 worth of clothes she was convicted of shoplifting and selling.

But the court said she should be allowed to deduct any money she spent on traveling to and from stores as well as storage and telephone costs at home.

The Jefferson Institute for Financial Independence

"Research indicates most business failures are the result of poor planning and undercapitalization," says Howard J. Ruff, the most influential financial advisor to America's middle class.

An entrepreneur in the truest sense, Ruff launched The Jefferson Institute for Financial Independence in 1986 to help other entrepreneurs succeed. It's an intensive, no-frills, down-to-business school for individuals serious about being in business for themselves.

In addition to an Entrepreneur Home Study course, the Institute offers an Entrepreneur Boot Camp aimed at the creation of a succinct, well-conceived, and well-executed business plan. Says Ruff, "Good business plans become blue prints for the future and, if done correctly, force the would-be entrepreneur to tend to seemingly insignificant details that can become major problems. Our motto is: *In With a Dream—Out With A Plan.*"

Because entrepreneurs usually lack the necessary capital to launch their ventures, Ruff also has formed a special Investor's Guild of individuals interested in investing in new businesses. Participants in the entrepreneur boot camp have the opportunity to get condensed versions of their business plans into the hands of every member of the Investor's Guild for evaluation. If it attracts interest, the entire business plan will be sent, and a meeting arranged with the potential investor.

The cost for the entrepreneur boot camp is not inexpensive, but serious entrepreneurs will look upon such cost as merely a small investment in their future.

FOOTNOTE: I participated in the 1986 Howard Ruff National Convention both as a workshop leader and member of Mr. Ruff's entrepreneur panel discussion, "Fulfilling the Dream of Financial Independence." This panel also included marketing genius Jay Abraham and Mark Stoddard, president of The Jefferson Institute. (This discussion was taped (both video and cassette) and copies may still be available from Ruff's organization, Target, Inc. (For Target's address, see *Ruff Times* in the periodical section of the resource chapter.

It was at this same convention that I met Dr. Gary North, who interviewed me for his series of "Firestorm Chats." I now offer a cassette tape of this 90-minute interview on the realities of a business at home.

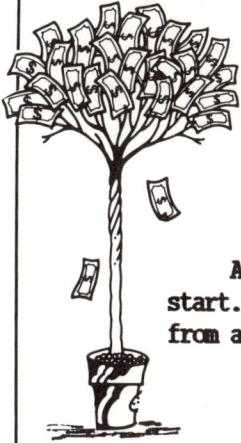

HOW TO GET THE MONEY FOR AN INDIVIDUAL RETIREMENT ACCOUNT

An IRA is one of the most important things a self-employed individual can start. It's never too late to start planning your first, or next, deposit. Here, from an investment firm in Wisconsin, are four ways to find the money for an IRA.

1. Borrow from your parents. There is a large portion of the work force that is starting out or raising a family and just doesn't have the $2,000 (or less) to invest. Their parents, however, may be 55-70, retired, or considering it. Many are in a position to give their children a tax-free gift of $2,000 (or less) and, in essence, provide their children with an IRA.

2. Have your employer deduct your IRA money from each paycheck, so you can be sure to have the money at the end of the year.

3. Borrow money from a bank or other institution to finance an IRA. An insurance policy may provide the asset needed for such a loan. Or, borrow from your pension plan. You would pay your own pension plan the interest and take a tax deduction on the interest paid. (Essentially, you would be paying yourself interest.)

4. Withdraw money from an existing IRA for 60 days to open a new IRA account. You are allowed one 60-day rollover every 12 months. You must, however, repay within 60 days the amount you've withdrawn, or pay taxes on that amount.

Other Tips

● Pay your spouse $2,000 for work done on your business, then put this earned income directly into a new IRA.

● Children can, and do, open IRAs, using money they've earned. Ask your banker how to establish such an IRA for your working children. (This is one way to let them help in building a college fund.)

● If you are unemployed, it may be worth the 10% penalty to use your IRA funds. Your tax bracket is low or nil until you find a new job, virtually eliminating taxes as well.

● Finally, always open your IRA on January 2 of each year to maximize the benefits of tax-free compounding. This can add up to substantial amounts over a period of years.

The above information was provided by Bruce Behling, Vice President of Strong Funds in Wisconsin. See the resource chapter to order the company's IRA Kit.

How IRA Contributions Add Up

The chart at right shows how much money you would have at the end of 5-30 years if you regularly contributed $2,000 a year to your own Individual Retirement Account.

In addition to building for your future, IRA investments help you keep more of your hard-earned home business profits. (See *Homemade Money* for details on how to legally avoid taxes through such strategies as hiring family members, IRAs, etc.)

IRA Account Growth
At 10% Interest, Compounded Monthly

Years To Retirement	Deposit $2,000/Year
5	$13,615
10	36,018
15	72,877
20	133,521
25	233,299
30	397,465

Notes

Avoiding
Legal Pitfalls

5.

In the preceding chapter, the emphasis was on making and
saving money. In this chapter, the information is designed to help
you avoid legal problems of many kinds, on both the local and
national level. All of these topics are discussed in *Homemade
Money*, of course; some in greater detail, others in less. Again,
remember that *NHBR* — and thus this book — is a companion
publication to *Homemade Money* and a continuing dialogue among my
readers.

The Better Business Bureau

Interesting story here. My small mention of the Better
Business Bureau in a back issue opened a real can of worms, as I'll
soon explain. First read the letter I received after my mention of
the BBB:

> *"In your newsletter...you state that once listed
> with the BBB, readers could state this fact in their mail
> order literature, thus adding more credibility to their
> business and customer guarantees. This is incorrect.*
>
> *"The symbol and name, 'Better Business Bureau,' are
> registered trademarks owned solely by the Council of
> Better Business Bureaus, Inc., and may NOT appear in any
> promotional sales, or other literature, or without
> express, written permission. The BBB cannot 'lend
> credibility' to an individual firm as they neither
> recommend nor deprecate any product, service, or
> company."*

The above letter was sent by the assistant manager of the BBB
office in the region where I lived at that time. After my mention
of this organization, a reader called her local office to double
check on whether she could mention the BBB in her mail-order
literature.

"I just wanted to make sure," she told me later. "The woman
in the BBB said she wasn't quite sure about this, but would get
back to me. I didn't hear from her for a couple of months. Then,
one night, while I was away from home, she stopped by to pick up

"Our local zoning laws came into question concerning the operation of a child care center in a home," writes a reader in Massachusetts.

"Paraphrased, the decision of the zoning board was: <u>unless the law says you can, you can't.</u>

"At a local women's business meeting, I heard my state representative, Sue Tucker, speak on 'Women and Business.' Although concerned about homebased business and its problems, she was unaware of how many business owners there were in her district.

"After hearing her speak, I decided to approach her. Since I was sewing and teaching at home illegally, both in the 'before and after' zoning laws, I needed her assurance that I would remain anonymous. Given that, I gave her copies of the model zoning ordinance from the NAHB, information about a local organization of homebased businesswomen, and a list of books. She passed these on to the board, called me for some clarification on some points, and we now have an acceptable law for town meeting.

"Through all this, Rep. Tucker kept her promise of confidence and motivated other women legislators to work with their communities to amend zoning laws to help homebased businesses. Our biggest disappointment was that these types of businesses are considered a 'women's issue' by her male counterparts. We MUST make our elected officials aware of us and out needs. Please continue to encourage your readership to write their legislators on all levels and to join and support home business organizations. I have...and I know it WORKS.

the original copy of your newsletter with this information. When I found out, I was furious! I didn't want to make a big deal out of this. She wouldn't give the newsletter back, and when I asked her to drop the matter, she got angry and said I had 'dragged myself into the matter.' Dragged myself into WHAT, I wanted to know? If this is how the BBB works, I want no part of it," my reader concluded.

As a result, my newsletter ended up in Washington, D.C. in the hands of management of the Council of Better Business Bureaus, Inc., who ordered my local BBB office to send the letter published above.

I'm glad this happened because it appears that a LOT of us—especially writers and editors—have misconceptions about the BBB. So here's the "straight scoop" at last.

First, the information I published originally was based on what I learned from a lengthy conversation with an individual in my local BBB office. I didn't just make it up. She was, apparently, as ill-informed about the policies of the BBB as my subscriber's contact. I have since learned, from a more knowledgeable authority, that *there are NO tangible benefits to be derived from REGISTRATION with your local BBB, and even MEMBERS receive only a plaque for their office wall and occasional written reports on companies they might want to deal with.*

The BBB seems paranoid about anyone even *mentioning* its name, and NO ONE can say — to promote their business or give it added credibility—*that they are a member, or even registered.* And Heaven help you if you mention the BBB in print.

Even my mention—which, ironically, was intended to PROMOTE the Better Business Bureau—was a violation of their trademark, they said, as they ordered me to "cease use of 'Better Business Bureau'" and implied legal action if I didn't.

To further clarify, although consumers who call the BBB for information about your business may *think* you more "credible" by the mere fact that you are registered, the BBB *denies that such registration adds to your "credibility."*

Although a consumer may get a favorable reply about you from the BBB (meaning no complaints on file), *the BBB denies that this is any kind of "reference" or "recommendation."*

So, even if home-business owners would be accepted for membership, they would derive questionable benefits at best. However, since it costs nothing to REGISTER with your local BBB — and may result in favorable information being passed on to customers in your area, do consider this action.

But don't tell anyone you've done it.

Zoning Problems of Homebased Business Owners

In the city of Rahway, New Jersey, the zoning ordinance used to allow home businesses, but in 1976 they simply struck from the ordinance the whole paragraph relating to home businesses, thereby making all of them illegal. A court case in 1981 prompted a committee to work on this problem and get the law restored to pre-1976 rulings.

In Wichita, Kansas, some home businesses are allowed, others aren't. For example, you can make arts and crafts, but you can't "manufacture or process anything" (though, in truth, if you *make* crafts, you are manufacturing them). You can't sell anything you don't make yourself, display a sign, conduct any business in the garage, or have an employee who doesn't live in your home.

Without question, hundreds of people in Wichita operate illegal homebased businesses today.

Writes Deborah Robinson from Arkansas: "After a complaint by the neighbor of a man who operates a wood framing business from his home in Springdale, the city council made the decision that permits for cottage industries in R-1 areas would not be renewed in 1986. I'm enclosing a copy of my article about the council decision which appeared in the *Northwest Arkansas Times* in Fayetteville, where I am employed as a reporter."

In her article, Deborah said that 68 permits were involved. The woodworker mentioned above was reported by a neighbor who objected to the noise from customers and parking of customer vehicles near the residence. The woodworker replied, "Whether you grant this license or not the noise will continue," adding that woodwork was a hobby of his.

The Mayor of Springdale asked that the home occupations ordinance be reviewed, but as one alderman put it, "There's about three different ways to cut this thing, and none of them is going to be pleasing to all the parties involved."

The following letter from another reader suggests that if neighbors don't turn you in to zoning authorities, your competition might. He writes: "Recently I read in our local newspaper about a home entrepreneur being stopped by a local citizen. Local law conceals the identity of the accuser in such cases, so he/she is faceless behind the shield of anonymity. I called the business woman and learned that she is sure the citizen who turned her in is a competitor, as her neighbors didn't even know her silk screening business existed. Her budding business doesn't have the capital to rent a building so she appears stifled in her attempt to promote the American economy with a home business venture.

What's happening in Chicago is probably indicative of what's happening in major cities across the country. Here, all homebased businesses are illegal, yet thousands now work at home, and colleges throughout the city regularly offer home-business courses. In the past, city officials have simply looked the other way, rather than tackle this debatable issues. Early in 1986, however, the zoning administrator asked Chicago's Mayor to present to the City Council an amendment to the zoning ordinance. A hearing was held, and among those in attendance were two of my networking friends, Janet Hansen, a home business owner who has had an interesting zoning experience, and Leslie MacDonald, Director of the small business center at Truman College in Chicago.

Leslie reported that when she and three other women came forward to testify, one of the councilmen remarked, "What do we have here, the Avon ladies?"

Their testimony obviously set everyone straight in short order, but this gives an indication of how some city councils are going to look upon proposed zoning changes. In the end, nothing was decided, except that an in-depth study of homebased businesses needs to be made. Meanwhile, people in Chicago who want to start homebased businesses are being encouraged to do so, even by city

A Look at Chicago's Proposed Amendment to the Zoning Ordinance

In addition to any license, registration, permit or certification required under the Municipal Code, a home occupation in Chicago shall be subject to the following standards (among others):

● *shall occupy no more than 20% or 500 sq. ft., whichever is less.*

● *no outside employee(s) or contracted agent(s) shall be engaged for services on the premises or dispatched from the premises.*

● *shall not involve the retail trading of goods, commodities, products or articles on the premises.*

Proposed changes to Chicago's zoning ordinance also include this new definition of "Home Occupation:"

"A 'home occupation' is an accessory use of a dwelling unit for gainful occupation by the resident(s) of the dwelling unit. A home occupation shall be carried out entirely within the principal building and shall be a secondary use clearly incidental to the use of the dwelling as a residence.

"Home Occupation includes, but is not limited to, the following: art studio, data processing, professional office of physician, dentist or accountant for consultation purposes only, and not for general practice, tutoring, or musical instruction limited to one pupil at a time."

Specifically excluded are barber shops & beauty salons, stables/kennels, real estate offices, restaurants and auto repair/servicing.

officials who mostly advise one to (1) keep a low profile; (2) avoid aggravating neighbors, and (3) pay applicable taxes. This is good advice no matter where you live.

Janet Hansen, owner of Koolewong, Ltd., has been waging her own small zoning war in her community of Mt. Prospect, a Chicago suburb. Her efforts to change zoning laws were discussed in a feature newspaper article that broadcast the illegality of her homebased business to everyone in the community. Later, she appeared in a CBS TV segment on working at home, further broadcasting the illegality of her own business. Curiously, nothing adverse has happened as a result of this visibility and Janet's many meetings with city officials. Everyone knows what she is doing, but no one is doing anything about it. It's almost as if this kind of visibility is a form of protection.

If zoning laws are preventing your homebased business from surfacing and growing through increased visibility, why don't you take up the sword in your town or city and do something about this problem? First try to get the names of as many homebased business owners as possible, so you will know whom to call on for support or testimony when the time is right.

Also speak to your elected officials, as suggested on page 60, to see if outdated zoning laws might be changed. Homebased businesses are a positive force, good for the economy of any community, but city officials will never change the law unless and until they are pressured by business owners to do so.

Commercial Kitchens & The Food Industry

The homebased business owner who decides to enter the food industry must be concerned not just with local zoning ordinances, but with local health officials and state regulations as well. (Local health authorities reportedly comb newspaper ads to spot unlicensed food services.) In fact, the law in your state may make it almost impossible to set up a food-related business in your home. Here, to give you an idea of what's involved in establishing a "commercial kitchen" required by the Health Department in any state, is a report from Sylvia Campbell Landman in California, who teaches home-business courses:

"So many of my people ran into confusion with food-handling permits that I did some research here and actually applied for a permit so I would receive a packet of all the regulations in my state.

"Just to apply for a permit, you must submit three sets of plans (to scale) of the intended work area. And you must submit three copies of equipment lists/prices, manufacturer's name/model numbers, along with separate drawings of the inside and outside of an exhaust hood, storage areas, all electrical connection plans, mopsink, etc. There is a fee of $250 for the plan review (not refundable, even if you are rejected), plus a yearly fee of $240.

"Most of my student caterers rent outside kitchens to get around the complicated regulations. Popular here are bakeries for use in the evening hours, and pizza parlor kitchens in the early a.m. One who met the state's requirement solved her problem by buying a storage building from Montgomery Ward, then put in the required sinks, two Coleman stoves, etc. to make her jams and jellies in her backyard." (Ed. note: Another of my readers reported that she solved her cake-baking problem by using the commercial kitchen in her church.)

A newspaper article sent by an Iowa reader indicates that this state also takes a dim view of homebased food service businesses. They not only regulate them tightly, but inspect them closely. Iowa's 50-pg. manual on this topic requires, among other things, that commercial kitchens be separate from the rest of the household, have a three-sink unit, and tile or linoleum floors.

A recent Iowa ruling does cater to small food businesses, however. The "home bakery provision" attempts to draw the line between commercial food businesses and small operations like bake sales and farmer's markets. *(It is possible that other states have similar home bakery provisions in their food laws.)* It allows home bakers to operate without a license if they earn less than $2,000 per year and agree not to advertise their products. (All business must come from word-of-mouth advertising.) This $2,000 limit prevents large quantities of foods prepared in uninspected kitchens from reaching the public, and those who buy from unlicensed home bakers must take the risk of food contamination upon themselves, according to the newspaper article.

In summary, then, be sure to investigate local and state laws thoroughly before launching or expanding any food-related business at home, and make sure you have some kind of liability insurance for even the smallest food-related hobby business. (See *Homemade Money* for more on the liability insurance topic.)

Possible Solution to Product Liability Insurance Problem

The owners of a party-plan business told me that product liability was a major consideration and obstacle in the establishment of their party-plan business. Insurance was not available in their area at a reasonable premium because they had no "storefront." Solution? They incorporated under Sub-chapter S — something you'll read about in the next article.

"This does not give us the product liability coverage we sought," my readers said, "but it does work to protect our personal and family properties. We were advised that, with the relative safety of our inventory, this should be adequate."

Do investigate incorporation as a means of protection for your homebased business, but understand that individuals who are responsible for wrongful acts will remain liable for those acts whether incorporated or not. In essence, a corporation protects personal assets only when your *employees or agents* are responsible for the business' liability.

Zoning Endnote

In Herndon, Virginia, a quilting teacher who decided to be aboveboard obtained the required personal service license and zoning permit which prohibits the following: signs, accessory buildings, displays, sales, consultation visits from clients for commissions, employees, and more than four students at a time, or more than eight in a day.

What's especially irritating to her is that she knows at least ten people who flagrantly violate the ordinance, either with students or sales. It's this kind of situation that often prompts people to enter complaints against neighbors and friends.

INCORPORATING WITHOUT A LAWYER

by Dorothea Kaplan

The corporation has become the most credible and least risky way to carry on business in our contemporary commercial climate, says Dorothea Kaplan, an attorney and author who believes in self-incorporation.

"Setting up the business corporation nowadays," she says, "has become so routine that entrepreneurs can easily complete the process for themselves without incurring substantial legal fees."

Recently, I led 50 people at a three-hour library seminar through the entire Illinois incorporation process. At the seminar's end, the participants had only to sign the Articles (Certificate) and send them off in duplicate to the Illinois secretary of state with the appropriate fees to complete the procedure. We've had equal success with our legal self-help audio cassette program on "Incorporating a Business in Illinois."

When contacting your secretary of state's office, Corporate Division, ask for blank pre-printed Certificates or Articles of Incorporation forms, a fee schedule, and all information available pertaining to the incorporation process in that state. Some states (such as New York and Nevada) will not have blank preprinted Certificate forms, but instead will forward a list of information to be included in self-prepared Certificates of Incorporation. The processing and servicing of corporations is big business and an important source of revenue in many states. You'll find all secretary of state offices efficient, prompt, and always cordial when handling your requests.

Advantages of Incorporation

Before plunging into the incorporation process, you ought to be familiar with the life processes of this fictional person and the advantages and disadvantage of doing business this way.

Ownership and management of the corporate entity are divided between the shareholders who own the company's proprietary interest and elect the board of directors, and the directors who formulate company policy and manage its affairs through the appointment of officers responsible for day-to-day operations. Company administrative rules are set out in the by-laws which are written by the shareholders or, if the shareholders wish, by the board of directors.

Regular business meetings must be held by the shareholders and by the directors. Records (or minutes) of all meetings are kept by the corporate secretary and maintained in the corporate minute book. The orderliness of the corporate processes must be maintained, otherwise the advantages that inure to the corporate business structure can be voided. These advantages fall into five categories:

● **Limited Liability of Shareholder.** The owner's or shareholder's liability is limited to his investment, while the sole proprietor or general partner risks not only his investment, but is responsible above and beyond that investment with his personal assets for all business debts and tort liability (injury to third persons) not sufficiently covered by insurance.

● **Continuity of Business.** The corporation's life is perpetual notwithstanding the death of a shareholder or the sale of his stock. In contrast, when the sole proprietor dies, or the partner dies or withdraws from a partnership, the disruption often causes the business to end.

● **Transferability of Ownership.** The corporate stock owner (except if you have a shareholder's agreement anticipating sale) freely conveys his proprietary interest by selling his shares to another party. Transfer of proprietor or partner ownership is complex and may even be prevented where, in a partnership, the remaining partner(s) won't accept the new person.

● **Management.** The board of directors is responsible for corporate policy decisions which are delegated to corporate officers for execution. In a proprietorship or partnership the owners wear all the decision-making hats. Since all partners have equal voices in policy formation, all are bound by each other's business decisions and are equally responsible for their execution.

● **Tax Advantages.** Both the sole proprietor and general partner must pass through all business income to their personal returns where individual tax rates often surpass corporate rates, especially for a smaller company.

Neither the partner nor proprietor can avail himself of nontaxable fringe benefits that the corporation can bestow upon its employees. Examples of nontaxable fringe benefits include a medical reimbursement plan, group term life insurance, wage continuation plan in event of disability, pension plans, and health and hospitalization insurance. Not only are these benefits nontaxable to the employee but the corporation receives an expense deduction for these, thereby reducing its own tax liability.

● **More Tax Advantages.** In addition to the above advantages, the Internal Revenue Code offers new corporations three other opportunities in the area of creative taxability:

S Corporation Status. If eligible and all shareholders (35 or less) agree by corporate resolution, the corporation can elect to be taxed as a partnership. The shareholders can then pass through all corporate losses, up to the amount of their capital contributions and loans on their personal returns, thereby reducing their personal tax liability. This is beneficial where the corporation expects high expenses and little income over the first several years of operation.

Losses on small business stock and amortization of organizational expenses are the other two tax advantages mentioned above.

Questions pertaining to all these topics should be directed to a lawyer specializing in the area of corporate taxation or an accountant knowledgeable in these areas.

Disadvantages of Incorporation

The disadvantages of incorporating are few and include the filing of two tax returns (personal and corporate), double taxation of dividends (personal and corporate), no limited liability where creditors require personal guarantees, added time for keeping corporate records, registration expenses when first organizing, and a yearly state minimum corporate tax of about $250 (called franchise tax in some states).

If you are incorporating a smaller business, there are services for hire which will, for fees below those charged by lawyers, maintain your corporate books, file annual reports, register assumed names, and do all the secretarial maintenance that is required to keep the corporate minutes book up to date.

Once the Certificate of Incorporation is completed in duplicate, it must be sent to the secretary of state, Corporate Division, in the state of incorporation, with a certified check for the appropriate filing fees (which may vary from $25 to over $100). After approval, the secretary's office will return a copy to you which must be filed in the county where the corporation's principal office will be located. Generally, the county recorder of deeds accepts these filings, charging fees from $10-$30 per Certificate.

Dorothea Kaplan is a Chicago area Attorney and founder of Law Lab, Inc., a legal self-help company. She is the author of Settle It Yourself—Who Needs a Lawyer, *the first book to offer 25 easy-to-use forms and special advice for making your own property damage, bodily injury, or accident claim against an insurance company. (See Resource Chapter to obtain her brochure or book.)*

A Few Words About Partnerships

Are you planning to start or dissolve a partnership? The following comments from three readers will alert you to pitfalls.

● Reader #1 ran into a problem when he formed an association with someone not as experienced in the business as he was. "Be sure you have the time to explain everything so the partner can follow through with the plans—not you," he advises. "When your reputation is on the line, it's hard to refrain from double-checking on your partner's activities."

● Reader #2 learned a bitter lesson about partnerships. Two years after she and her husband had dissolved a partnership with another person, the IRS came in and levied their bank account—right at the time they were trying to refinance a loan. Why? "Our former partner had not paid his income taxes for the past two years," my reader told me. "IRS can levy ANY partner's account for uncollected funds—even the account of the partner who did pay his share. A person learns real quick how helpless they are with government agencies such as IRS," she said.
Note: In dissolving a partnership, see if you can build into the dissolution contract some kind of safeguard against this kind of tax problem. No one wants a surprise like this two or three years after a partnership has been dissolved.

● Reader #3 sent this report after she bought out her partner: "When we had trouble coming to terms, we enlisted the aid of our accountant. He asked us for (1) inventory totals (equipment, raw materials and readymades), (2) accounts payable, and (3) accounts receivable to come up with net worth. He didn't state any values, but had us come in and hash out what we each felt was fair.
"We settled on a net worth of $40,000. I am, therefore, paying a total of $20,000 over a three-year period; $3,000 was paid at signing of contract. Equal payments of the balance will be made each quarter through 1987. I also took out declining term insurance to cover the contract in case anything happened to me before the balance was paid in full.
"Partnership dissolvement is somewhat like a divorce in that neither person wants to get shafted by the other! I would suggest that anyone looking for a business partner think ahead, asking what would I do if...? A partner may die or want out of the business, or you may want to buy out your partner.

Note: By law, at the death of a partner, a business is dissolved and can no longer operate until it is either liquidated or reorganized. In forming a partnership, a Buy-Sell Agreement can be established, funded by life insurance. The agreement, prepared by an attorney, establishes the price the survivor will pay for his share of the business, and that the heirs will sell for, and the insurance provides the money to complete the transfer. (Taken from *Homemade Money*.)

The Celebrity Rights Act

Your state may or may not have a Celebrity Rights Act now, but that will not protect you from a lawsuit if you are caught selling unlicensed products and services that utilize the name, voice, signature, photograph or likeness of any deceased personality. The following information will answer questions about this law. I first learned of it when I received a press release accompanied by a copy of Senate Bill 613, which California signed into law in 1984.

Several state now have statutes which prevent the merchandising of deceased personalities, including Florida, Nebraska, Oklahoma, Utah, Virginia and California. The California law follows a stricter June, 1984 Tennessee law and recent court decisions in New York, New Jersey, Florida and Georgia.

It specifically prohibits any person or company — without permission — from: (1) producing a product, (2) advertising a product, or (3) providing a service which in any way utilizes the name, voice, signature, photograph or likeness of a deceased person during a period lasting 50 years after their death.

How does this law affect the average craftsperson? I recall a crocheter who designed a "Marilyn Monroe Doll" for sale to her mail order customers. If she's still selling this particular doll or its pattern, she's inviting legal trouble.

My husband has a handpainted plaster bust of W. C. Fields hanging in his office. The company that made it, and the retailer who sold it, probably violated the above law without knowing it. Such replicas cannot be made without special permission from the estate of W. C. Fields. Note that the Celebrity Rights Act affects not only the manufacturer or creator of an unlicensed product or service, but distributors and retailers as well. *All* can be sued, according to the owner of Roger Richman Productions, Inc. the Los Angeles agency that represents the heirs and estates of such personalities, as Marilyn Monroe, Clark Gable, W. C. Fields, the Marx Brothers, Abbott & Costello, Carole Lombard, Mae West and others. This agency was, in fact, instrumental in having the California legislation enacted.

In a conversation with Richman, I learned that his agency plans to "go after violators in earnest." I asked how the law worked if one happened to live in a state without a celebrity rights act. He said that not all states need an act because there simply aren't enough celebrities in some states to warrant it. But regardless of whether there is a state law or not, you may be sure that, somewhere, there is an attorney or agency looking out for the rights of deceased personalities.

Here's an A-to-Z list of commercial uses affected by this Act: advertising, animation, apparel, barware, calendars, ceramics, collectibles, dolls, domestics, figurines, games, gifts, handcrafts, jewelry, lithographs, look-alike services, mirrors, mugs, office supplies, party goods, photographs, premiums, prints, promotions, publishing, records, reproductions, sound-alikes, souvenirs, stationery, syndication, textiles, timepieces, toys, t-shirts, video cassettes, wax museums, wall decor, and all other general uses mentioned above.

Uses excepted from the bill are: plays, books, magazines, newspapers, musical compositions, films, radio or television programs, political and newsworthy material, single and original works of fine arts and certain advertisements.

In the event you want to obtain a license to use a particular personality's characterization in some way, Richman suggests you contact the Screen Actor's Guild or the Academy of Motion Picture Arts and Sciences in Los Angeles.

INSIGHT INTO THE WORLD OF LICENSING

by Kathy Wirth & Dianne Davis

"Our experience deals with obtaining a license to adapt artist Charley Harper's work into needlework. We believe the same procedures, with a few adjustments, would apply to any field," say Kathy and Dianne, owners of KD Artistry, Inc., a needlework design company. This article, an outline of the plan they used, shares their special insight into the world of lawyers, licensing, and royalties.

Prove Yourself

Samples. Have samples of your work to show what you do and how well you do it. We graphed a simple Harper design and stitched it before meeting with him.

Experience: Show your experience in your field. We had fifteen designs of Cincinnati landmarks already on the local retail market.

Test Market: Prove there is a market for your product. We produced nine Harper designs in cross stitch and needlepoint and introduced them to the public at a local needlework fair.

Legal Aspects

Lawyers: Choose a lawyer you can talk easily with, and who does not intimidate you. We felt that if our lawyer had not been with a prestigious firm we would have been at a disadvantage in dealing with the artist's equally prominent law firm.

Fees: Lawyer's fees vary widely. Ask how they charge, a flat fee or by the hour. Usually you are charged for every phone call and letter. Some expensive lawyers and firms will give you a price break knowing that someday your little business will become a big business.

Dress for Success. Look like a business person. Even though we usually were more casual, when meeting with the lawyers, we followed the rules of business dressing. Seems silly, but it works.

Do your homework. Before the first visit with your lawyer, learn as much as you can about royalties common to your field, and how other companies deal with licensors. Also know what specifications are important to you and what restrictions you can live with.

License Agreement

Royalties. Royalties can vary within the same contract. Royalties on one product may be different than on another. Often a minimum royalty or an advance is required.

Term. Allow enough time to design, produce, and market your product. If your contract requires a minimum royalty at the end of a certain period of time, you may end up in the hole if it takes longer to get into production and set up a network of distribution.

Contract Renewal. It is best to have automatic renewal of your contract rather than having to reevaluate and renegotiate at the end of each time period.

Termination. Know how and why the license could be terminated. What are the steps that may lead to termination? Work out what will happen in the event of death of either licensor or licensee.

Understanding. Make sure you understand everything about the agreement, so that you won't have to be in constant touch with your lawyer.

Right of First Refusal. In the future, you or the licensor may want to branch out into other related fields. You should be allowed first chance at the opportunity to expand into a different area of business. If you decline, the opportunity may then be offered to others.

Copyright ownership. Copyright your work— list your copyright and the licensor's copyright if necessary.

Territory. The world is getting smaller all the time, so name the territory in which you can sell. No need to limit yourself to a small area. Look out world, here we come!

CONSUMER PRODUCT SAFETY GUIDELINES

For Makers of Toys, Children's Articles, and Clothing

The following letter was received in response to one of my articles in *Crafts* magazine, which briefly discussed various federal laws and regulations applicable to craft sellers (as included in my books). Christine Nelson of the U. S. Consumer Product Safety Commission in Washington, DC has provided detailed information which will be helpful to many.- Editor.

I was pleased to see your article about federal regulations and the Consumer Product Safety Commission (CPSC) address where people can write for more information. We will be glad to supply your readers with copies of our regulations for toys, children's articles and clothing.

There are some clarifications I wish to make about CPSC regulations as they apply to crafts. The majority of regulations which apply to toys and children's articles were promulgated under the Federal Hazardous Substances Act. Those regulations which I believe would be of special interest to craftspeople are:

1. The small parts requirement which prohibits small parts which could be a choking hazard in toys and articles for children under three years of age.

2. The sharp edge and sharp point requirements which describe tests for identifying hazardously sharp edges and points in toys and articles for children under 8 years of age.

3. Requirements for rattles to ensure that the ends or handles of rattles are large enough so they cannot enter a child's mouth and throat and cause choking.

4. Flammability requirements for toys state a limit on the burning rate. (Toys which pass this test may still ignite and burn, but they will not burn explosively).

As you pointed out in your article, the Federal Hazardous Substances Act also addresses products that are toxic, corrosive, an irritant or a strong sensitizer. We find that these types of hazards are rare among toys and children's articles. Small parts, sharp points and edges and noncomplying baby rattles are by far the more frequent hazards we see among toys and children's products.

Beware of Surface Coatings Which Contain Lead

Under the Consumer Product Safety Act there is a ban of paint and other surface coatings, such as varnish, lacquer and shellac, which contain more than 0.06% lead by weight. *We have no objection to the use of paint or other surface coatings on children's products as long as they comply with the lead-in-paint-ban.* Paints sold for household use in the United States must comply with this ban. Only paints intended for specialized uses are exempt. Such paints must bear a label which warns that the paint contains lead, may be harmful if eaten or chewed and should not be applied to toys, children's articles or furniture.

NOTE: Artist's paints are exempt from the lead-in-paint ban but are not required to bear a warning label regarding lead.

The Flammability Requirement

As indicated in your article, it is difficult to tell by looking at a fabric if it is "so highly flammable as to be dangerous." The quick test you suggest may help to identify fabrics that comply with the children's sleepwear standard, *if the match is held on the bottom edge of a small piece of fabric for approximately three seconds.* If the fabric stops burning once the match is removed from the fabric, it is "self-extinguishing" and will probably comply with the children's sleepwear standard — *a very stringent flammability standard. (More, over)*

If the fabric continues to burn, it will not comply with the children's sleepwear standard, but will probably comply with the flammability standard for all other fabrics intended for use in wearing apparel, doll clothing and toys. *Most fabrics comply with this latter standard,* but it is difficult to make a determination of compliance by setting a match to a small piece of fabric held vertically because acceptance is based upon both the ease of ignition and the rate of burn. During the test, the fabric is held in a less stringent position (at a 45-degree angle, rather than vertical), and the flame touches the fabric in a less ignitable location (the top surface instead of the bottom edge).

Check Supplier's Invoice
For Compliance Statement

We would suggest that a craft seller check the supplier's invoice if buying from a manufacturer, wholesaler or distributor for a statement of compliance with the federal flammability standards, or contact the supplier and ask for a guaranty of compliance with the applicable flammability standard. Most fabric manufacturers test their fabrics for compliance with the standards and issue a guaranty of compliance. This guaranty is generally passed along the chain of distribution by using an invoice statement, *"Continuing guaranty under the Flammable Fabric act filed with the Consumer Product Safety Commission."*

If the fabric used by a craft seller is being purchased at local retail outlets, we would suggest contacting the fabric manufacturer directly or calling the CPSC to see if the fabric manufacturer has filed a continuing guaranty.

Editor's note: See the resource chapter for the address of the CPSC, which will send additional information upon request.

Now That's "Evidence"

A publisher friend, who prefers to remain anonymous, shared this little "legal story" which has a good punch line at the end. She writes:

"I took a business law course in grad school, and used to rant and rave over different decisions we studied. But that isn't fair, I would say. The professor always answered: "This isn't a course in justice, it's a course in *law*." Another of his favorite statements was "...the party with the most written evidence wins."

So...I sold $2,000 worth of handmade merchandise to a well-known New York company in April, 1982. Biggest order I'd ever had, and I was proud. They reordered in November, but as they hadn't paid, I didn't send the order. In December, one of the buyers admitted in writing that they had sold all my merchandise and wanted more before Christmas. "I'll send it as soon as you pay for the last order," was my answer.

TWO YEARS WENT BY, during which time I received only one check for $26. I kept writing letters to all the officers of the company. I visited their accounting department in person twice during that time, on trips when I was in New York anyway. After each visit, I wrote letters reiterating what they had said. Several times they asked for copies of all my account sheets I always sent just what they asked for—but only photocopies.

The tone of my early letters was businesslike, but toward the end I started saying "I can't believe you are doing this to me...that you would sell all my goods and not pay me."

The letters got more personal and I told them what their not paying was doing to my little company. I told them my problems, and how many hours it takes to make a product. *What I was doing was building up written evidence.*

By the time I finally said I would sue them, I was writing real tear-jerker letters. They sent the check in full.

I'm convinced that when their lawyer or business manager looked over the file of letters, they decided they would look very bad in court. I think that being sued is an everyday occurrence to them, so that was no threat at all. But a file full of letters like that? *That's EVIDENCE.*

Common-Law Trademarks—More Powerful Than You Think

If you have a copy of *Homemade Money*, you know that attorney Mary Helen Sears has verified for accuracy the information on copyrights, patents, and trademarks.

About a year after the book was published, I talked with her again, discussing the name of my periodical and the fact that I do not have a federal registration of my "mark," which is both the name of *National Home Business Report*, and the way it is written. What I learned may be helpful to you.

As my subscribers have probably noticed, the name carries the letters "TM" after it. Companies and businesses which have not yet filed for a federal trademark often use these letters to indicate they have claimed a mark. But you can use the "TM" even if you have no intention of registering for a federal trademark. Actually, you establish your trademark simply by using it in interstate commerce.

If you are the first to use a mark this way, you automatically acquire a *common law trademark.* Even without federal registration of such a mark, you could probably stop someone else from using it, says Ms. Sears. A common law trademark has more power than you might imagine. However, Ms. Sears adds that it is much easier to fight an effective court battle if your mark has been registered with the U. S. Patent & Trademark Office.

When I named my periodical, I deliberately attached my name to the periodical's name in the belief that even if another publisher did select a similar name, there would be little chance of confusion in the minds of prospective subscribers. After all, all four words of my newsletter name are generic, and this alone would make federal registration difficult to obtain.

According to an article by Thomas M. S. Hemnes in the March/April 1985 issue of *Harvard Business Review*..."a word or a combination of words that describes a product will not be protected as a trademark and cannot be registered on the Principal Register of the United States Patent and Trademark Office unless it has acquired a secondary meaning. A descriptive word or phrase is said to have acquired a secondary meaning if, through long and exclusive use by one person, it has come to be associated with that person so that it indicates the source of goods and not merely the type."

I interpret this to mean that, the longer I use the phrase, "*Barbara Brabec's National Home Business Report,*" the stronger my common law trademark becomes, and the stronger my case for claiming that a "secondary meaning" has been established.

Two questions immediately come to mind at this point, however. One, why go to the time and expense of trying to obtain a federal registration for my mark if I already have a strong common law trademark established? Two, if someone actually infringed on my mark (either common law or federally-registered), would I actually want to engage in an expensive court battle to fight the infringer?

These are questions you may also be asking yourself. If you have a trademark experience you'd like to share with me and my readers, I'd like to hear from you.

Trademark Search Service

A reader sent the following information in July 1984. The prices mentioned may be out of date, but the service is apparently

"Here are two tips on copyright," begins a note from Judiann in California.

"In our area, the phone book has a page of federal and government phone numbers. One of the listings is the Federal Information Center. By calling this number, you may request copyright forms and pamphlets. And you'll probably have the forms in a couple of days. When writing the Copyright Office, it can take six weeks or longer.

"The other hint is that the Copyright Office will accept your 'collections' bound with a plastic report cover, found in stationery stores."

Editor's Note: *Judiann is referring to the fact that, instead of copy-righting designs on an individual basis, you can submit them as a "collection" or simple booklet. I recall one designer who photocopied her collection of designs at the local print shop, had the printer punch holes in the set of pages, and then added a cover (designed for the occasion). She then bound her collection as a book, using heavy thread. It worked fine.*

"Recently, in one of my 'Designer Sweatshirts' classes at a shop in southern Minnesota," writes Mary Mulari, "I noticed a packet of information and designs for sale on the topic of decorating sweatshirts, which is also the subject of my first book, Designer Sweatshirts.

"Since I am basically curious by nature and always interested in what the competition is publishing, I purchased the packet. It was a shock to recognize my own diagrams, illustrations and designs, as well as my text only slightly reworded. No one had ever asked for permission to use my materials, so I knew this was an infringement of my copyright. My information and drawings had been stolen and now were being offered by another company at a price much lower than my own book.

"I found an attorney and he informed the company publishing the packet that I was aware of their use of my materials and that they should cease selling their packet or face a trial.

"The first response from the company was to pay me royalties. From that point, we were able to work out an agreement which includes royalties, their payment of my attorney's fees and written information in each packet crediting me for the information and listing my name and address. A court trial was avoided.

"This experience has shown me the importance of keeping in touch with the marketplace and with other publications, as well as the value of registering a copyright. Self-publishers must stay on their toes!"

still in existence, and you'll find the firm's address in the resource chapter if you want to follow up on it:

"If you're willing to pay," says my reader, "Government Liaison Services, Inc. will search a name for copyright or trademark for $80 (two for $150), and call you collect within just a couple of days to tell you if it's available or taken. And they know all the rules and what will probably process and what won't.

"This firm will process your application for a trademark ($150) and virtually guarantee immediate processing. Then, if you have a symbol, they will do the art work properly (lower third of the page, proper ink, etc.) for about $60. I think the expense is worthwhile if you really are in a hurry to know."

A Little Copyright Story

You'll find considerable information on copyrights in *Homemade Money;* what follows are merely tidbits adding to this information.

A woman decided to modify a pattern she had purchased, and offer it for sale in a crafts magazine. She called the advertising department of that magazine and told them she wanted to advertise a pattern that was based on someone else's design. "It's okay...as long as you've made a few changes," she was advised.

So the woman took her savings to pay for the ad, and upon publication, a friend of the original designer's saw the ad and sent her a copy.

Whereupon the original designer contacted her lawyer, who in turn informed the advertiser that she had infringed on a copyrighted pattern and must stop selling it immediately. Further, all proceeds from the ad had to be directed to the original designer.

MORAL OF STORY: To be safe, be original. And *never* take advice on important matters unless the person giving it is an authority on the topic.

How to Stop Illegal Copying

See the sidebar material in this section for information on how one designer handled infringement of her copyright, and other related notes from readers.

One way to prevent the average consumer from photocopying copyrighted material is to use a special paper made by Boise Cascade called "Cascade Hidden Void." (Your printer or paper supply house can give you ordering information.) When copied, this paper shows the word "VOID" diagonally across the page.

Another technique designers have used, when charting cross stitch graphs, is to print patterns in red and black, which means the photocopied design will indicate no separation of colors, since both red and black reproduce as black. Similarly, charts could be printed in non-reproducible blue ink—the kind I used to create the "boards" for this book. The blue lines show where to paste columns, but are not picked up by the camera's eye.

This copying problem may seem insignificant to some people, but to professional designers in the crafts/needlecraft industry, it's very disturbing. Says one, "The general public must be made to know that paying a few dollars for a booklet, magazine, pattern or craft fair ornament does not give them the right to exactly duplicate and profit from what may have taken the artist years to develop. I've done only a few fairs, but I've had customers tell me they were going to make 100 copies of my ornaments for a bazaar, but not to worry because it was in another state! That helped me get out of the fair business and back into selling to magazines and craft companies where, if I was illegally copied, at least I'd earn more than $5 or a 'free look' for my designs. Crafts is supposed to be a *creative* business. People who only copy others won't get far—and if they try, they're only going to get into trouble."

A Few Notes on Patents

Most of the feedback I've had from my readers suggests that patents are something the average small business person should avoid. "I found a patent/copyright attorney, made an appointment, and came away feeling depressed," one reader told me. "He thought my idea was good and marketable, and he said he'd be willing to help, but it would be costly and time consuming. He said a search would need to be done ($300-400) and a pamphlet prepared with illustrations and all the legals, to the tune of $1,500-$3,000, and maybe as much as two years of time. His advice was: Select a company name, register that; design and trademark a label, and produce the item myself.

He also told me, 'If it's a good item or a hot item, it's just a matter of whoever gets there (on the market) first with the most, because 15 minutes after it hits the public market, it will be stolen, changed a little, and produced in mass quantities. If you want to make money, you have to do it first, be first, and fight like crazy to STAY first.'"

Actually, the above prices seem low, based on what a patent attorney quoted in a recent workshop I attended. He said it usually costs between $5,000-$20,000 to obtain a patent, and even when you have a patent, you can't be sure of keeping it, or even using it. (Conceivably, you could patent something only to find that a prior patent existed, automatically making yours null and void. Patents are not always in file when a patent search is underway.)

See *Homemade Money* for additional information on patents, and remember that it takes a lot of time and money to both enter the marketplace with a patented item, then protect your investment once you've begun to sell. As many novice patent holders have learned, defending a patent in court is beyond the means of the average small business owner, particularly if a big-bucks company is the one who has stolen the idea.

The Trouble With Independent Contractors

As small business people, we often rely on independent contractors to help us develop and expand our homebased businesses. But many people do not understand the legal difference between an "employee" and an "independent contractor," nor do they realize the financial implications of using the latter improperly.

In *Homemade Money*, you'll find the Supreme Court Guidelines on the difference between these two categories of workers, along with a complete discussion of the labor department law that prohibits the hiring of homebased workers as independent contractors in the garment industry. I don't want to get into a lengthy discussion of

How to Investigate the Copyright Status of a Work

You'll find the address of the Copyright Office in the resource chapter. For information on how to make a search of the Copyright Office catalogs, or have the Copyright Office make a search for you, ask for Circular R22.

"Several years ago my husband developed a puzzle and went through the excitement of getting a patent on it," a woman told me. " A few months later, before he had time to get it marketed, I walked into one of our better stores in the area and gasped! There was my husband's puzzle on a beautiful display. It was like someone had hit me in the chest with a baseball bat. Consequently, I paid $10 for the puzzle and ran home to show my husband.

"As we found out—too late—big companies are always watching patents, and they saw this one and copied it, changing it so slightly only my husband could tell. Two professors from Cornell University came into the picture as a result of this, wanting to help my husband sue the company. But he's a very creative man, so his response was that he'd just come up with something better. Now he has, and this time he's planning to get it copyrighted, not patented. And we're being very cautious."

How to Avoid Insurance Problems with Contract Workers

The following "contract worker agreement" was suggested by an insurance agent who was questioned about the topic of possible insurance problems with independent contractors:

Contract Worker Agreement

As an independent contractor, I fully understand that I am not an employee of (your company name). Therefore, any expenses that I incur while rendering my services to (company) are my responsibility. Also, (company) is not responsible for any injuries received while completing an assigned contract.

In addition, (company) is not liable for federal and state withholding taxes and/or employee benefits for services contracted by them.

Date: _____
Name (signature)
Social Security Number
Address/phone

this topic here, because it is possible that by the time this book is published the law will be changed. In spite of this, however, several thriving cottage industries involved in making women or children's garments were in the process of being sued by the Department of Labor in December, 1986 because of pressure from the Garment Worker's Union. Watch *NHBR* for updates on this topic.

Meanwhile, if you are using independent contractors for any purpose, check to make sure you're on safe legal ground. It is *not* enough for an accountant (or even an attorney) to say, "Sure, you can consider them an independent contractor," because not all accountants and attorneys are well versed in labor law. And you are not going to be safe just because the person you hire tells you, "Sure, you can pay me on an independent contractor basis," meaning they'll take care of their own taxes. If in fact that person works for you on a regular basis throughout the year, and meets other guidelines applicable to an employee, as laid down by the Supreme Court, he or she is, in truth, an employee, and you would be responsible for back taxes even though you had been paying wages on an independent contractor basis. In summary, then, merely *saying* someone is an independent contractor does not make it so, and using workers on an improper basis does not relieve an individual from the usual responsibilities of an employer.

I have been told that one way to be safe in hiring outside help is to use individuals who are also self-employed, and provide services to several other businesses. Your argument that the people you hire are, in fact, independent contractors, might have extra weight if you get such individuals to sign a "Contract Worker Agreement" shown at left. An insurance agent suggested it to one of my readers, who shared it with the *NHBR* readership.

Possible Problem in the Computer Industry

Thousands of people who have purchased computers in order to process data for business customers see themselves as "independent contractors." But, in mid-1985, the Internal Revenue Service ruled that many people who work at home using their own word processors are, in fact, "employees."

Because it is easier for companies to work with people like this (they don't have all the paperwork regarding withholding taxes, unemployment insurance, social security, etc.), they naturally encourage individuals in this regard.

It appears, then, that the IRS could easily challenge such "independent contractors" on the basis that the investment in a small computer is not a "substantial investment" in equipment; thus they do not meet the legal requirements for independent contractors. IRS is apparently taking the stand that small computers, being almost as common as typewriters, are nothing special. Therefore, if you hire such people on this basis, you'd be wise to consult an expert to avoid possible tax problems in the future. And, if you're working for some company on this basis, you may be losing out on some employee benefits you're legally entitled to receive, such as paid vacations and medical insurance.

See *Homemade Money* for additional information on patents, and remember that it takes a lot of time and money both to enter the marketplace with a patented item, and protect your investment once you've begun to sell. As many novice patent holders have learned, defending a patent in court is beyond the means of the average small business owner, particularly if a big-bucks company is the one who's stolen the idea.

Marketing Makes the Difference

6.

With a sound business idea, some common sense and a little up-front money, almost anyone can launch a small business at home if they have even the barest business know-how to begin with. Ah, but *staying* in business...there's the rub. It doesn't take long for the novice to realize there's a lot more to financial success than a good idea and a willingness to work hard.

An understanding of the business topics discussed in *Homemade Money* and earlier chapters of this book is only part of the picture. What most small business owners need most—and often resist the longest—is an entrepreneur's education in marketing. Ironically, even a business-school graduate can be lacking in this department, as evidenced by this letter from a *NHBR* reader in California:

> *"I have a growing line of patterns which I initially sold mail order and now wholesale to retail shops. I will never be really successful at this until I can get my patterns into more stores nationwide. How can I find good sales reps in other parts of the country?*
>
> *"The really agonizing part of this is that I have a Bachelor's degree in business (marketing major), graduated with honors, and am beginning work on my MBA this fall. The truth is, business schools work to turn out good employees, not good entrepreneurs. The nuts-and-bolts RULES of business are not mentioned in business school. It's assumed 100% of graduates will go to work for someone else who's already figured it out. A marketing major is trained to be a salesperson. I was taught to sell but learned nothing about the channels of distribution, advertising, or sources of supply for businesses outside of the Fortune 500. It is expected you will learn these things on your way up the corporate ladder in your chosen industry."*

Most small business owners learn about marketing the hard way, by making expensive mistakes that teach them what *not* to do the next time around; like placing display ads in the wrong publications, going to trade shows without a knowledge of industry pricing structures or channels of distribution, or offering the right product or service to the wrong audience, and vice versa.

> *"The purpose of a business is not to make profits but to create and keep customers,"* says Theodore Levitt, author of *The Marketing Imagination* (The Free Press, Div. of Macmillan, Inc.)
>
> And: *"It's not the product that makes the sale, it's the savvy that makes the market."*

Notes

Often, the most expensive mistakes are the ones made as a result of hasty decisions based on inadequate market research or knowledge about one's industry. Such business ignorance, coupled with a lack of self-confidence or a fear of losing sales (or not getting customers at all) may also cause novice business owners to charge much less than the market will actually bear, making business survival almost impossible to begin with.

If you've never taken the time to create a marketing plan for your business, I urge you to do it now. In the process of putting your marketing problems on paper, along with all your thoughts and ideas on how to overcome them, you'll automatically gain a better understanding of your product or service, your industry, your prospective buyers or clients, and what you've got to do to get ahead financially. A written marketing plan may also show you exactly what you've been doing wrong in the past.

It's never too late to take a new step toward financial success, and it's not that difficult to write a simple plan. In fact, if you'll just answer the questions listed below, jotting brief answers in the margins of this book, you'll already have the beginnings of a useful marketing tool that will enable you to develop new marketing strategies for your business.

Outline For a Simple Marketing Plan

● **What do I do?** (Write a description of your business in 25 words or less.)

● **How does my product or service _benefit_ buyers?** (Remember that people do not buy products or services per se, they buy the _benefits_ offered by those products or services—savings of time or money, peace of mind, happiness, self-confidence, and so on.)

● **How do I want to be perceived by my buyers or clients?** (Thinking in terms of the benefits you offer buyers—the problems you help them solve, or the needs you satisfy—create a 7-word statement that will properly _position you in the minds of your prospects._ Your continued use of this statement (or variations of it) in all your promotional and advertising copy will help create the image you want people to have of you and your business.)

> (**EXAMPLE:** In a 25-word description of my business, I might say that "I write, publish, and sell my own books, publish a quarterly report for homebased business owners, and present seminars and workshops across the country." My 7-word positioning statement, however, is this: "I help people succeed in homebased businesses.")

● **What are the characteristics of my target audience?** (Indicate age, income, lifestyle, geographic location, etc., along with whatever your market research information to date tells you about the total number of potential customers in your target area, the share of the market you expect to capture, and why.)

● **Who is my competition?** (Write a description of your competitor/s, what you think their share of the market is, what you think their strengths and weaknesses are, what they might do to take business away from you, and how you'd fight back.)

● **How will I market my product or service?** (Will you sell to the private sector or to the business community, and will you deal with buyers or clients directly or indirectly; retail or wholesale, market by mail, through reps, trade shows, and so on. Also, can you franchise your business?)

● **How will I advertise, and where?** (Display ads in magazines, classified ads in local papers, circulars, direct marketing by mail, trade ads or shows, conventions, etc. Also consider your publicity opportunities—see the publicity chapter in this book for some good ideas.)

● **What are my selling policies?** (You'll need to establish standard credit terms, guaranties, customer discounts, returns policy, shipping or delivery charges, and so on.)

● **Is my pricing okay?** (Is it in line with industry standards? Does the present economy in your market area justify higher or lower prices for certain products or services in your line? How do your prices compare to that of your competitors? If lower, are you sure you can make a profit after all costs are considered...and do you really want to accept anything less than what your competition gets? If your prices are higher, can you justify them by offering something special your competition does not? Why might your prospects gladly pay a higher price for what you offer? Again, think of the *benefits* you offer).

You've got the idea by now. After creating your first rough-draft marketing plan, you'll have something to build on. And, as you gain additional marketing information and expertise, you'll begin to fully understand how better marketing automatically leads to greater income. As you read the following articles and marketing information gleaned from back issues of *National Home Business Report*, remember that a subscription to this periodical will bring you an continuing supply of business and marketing information you can use in the day-to-day operation of your homebased business.

MARKETING BEGINS WITH A VISION

by Herman Holtz

Two young men had a vision. They saw a great gap in the computer market: no one was making and selling really small and inexpensive computers to small businesses and other such users. But recent technological breakthroughs in microelectronics had made such a computer possible. They decided to act on their their vision, their first factory the garage adjoining the home of one of the two. That vision and humble beginning produced the Apple computer and the large company that produces and sells it today.

Others with such visions created the Xerox Corporation, IBM, and many other great companies. But it is not only those with visions of new and different products who produce successes. Jack Miller had a vision of an office-products firm which would give better service to its customers than others did, and he also started in his own home—his basement—to create the large Quill Corporation of today.

How to Be a Visionary

The vision is the beginning of marketing. (sales activity comes later.) It has two necessary ingredients: something to sell (an offer) and someone to sell it to (buyers). Every successful enterprise is based on a beginning idea, but the idea must include these two items as the initial ingredients. You can hardly expect to sell anything if you are not precisely sure what it is that you are selling and to whom you are offering it—who it is who ought to buy it.

It's never too late to have that vision. Even after you have begun, you can ponder what it is that you are trying to sell, and to whom you are trying to sell it. Far better to discover this late, than not at all. Even large corporations, such as Robert Hall and Korvette's, fail when they stop pondering this and begin to try to force their merchandise down the public's throat—when they abandon the original vision that made them successful in the first place.

Surveys of success among business and industrial entrepreneurs revealed one highly relevant common trait: almost without exception, successful entrepreneurs said it was not money per se

that was their prime motivator, but doing whatever it was they set out to do better than it had ever been done before. Xerox began when the tiny Halide Corporation was the first to listen to the inventor of the xerographic copying system, after so many others had laughed at his invention. Halide had the vision, and they never abandoned it. They continue to bring out new and better service than anyone else in their business, and they never permit that to deteriorate.

Don't Make Sales, Make Customers

The true objective of every business enterprise is not to make sales, but to create customers. In fact, many enterprises lose money on their first sale or even on second and third sales to a given customer, because it has cost them so much money to gain that customer. The only way they can turn a profit on that customer and, therefore, in their business overall, is to keep that customer coming back for more and recommending them to other customers.

Recognizing that it costs a great deal of money to create a customer, is it not self-protection to do whatever is necessary to keep that customer? To provide good products, good service, courtesy, guarantees, and prompt adjustment of complaints? (And is that not marketing, since it is all aimed at making sales, which is the final act of marketing?)

If your enterprise is not built on a vision, start working on one. Think out who your proper customer prospects are, why they should buy what you offer, and how you can give them the best of products and service. Do that, stick to it, and have faith in your vision.

Herman Holtz is an independent consultant and the author of more than thirty business books, including The Secrets of Practical Marketing for Small Business *(Prentice-Hall),* Mail Order Magic *and* Persuasive Writing *(both published by McGraw-Hill). See author's listing in the resource chapter.*

Do you have the Courage to Make Changes?

"Change requires awareness," says Herman Holtz in his excellent book, *The Secrets of Practical Marketing for Small Business.* "You must keep up, know your industry, know what's happening in the marketplace."

Change is inevitable, but it requires courage, stresses Herman. Timid, fearful businesspeople tend to cling to the old ways stubbornly, irrationally, and *fatefully.*

Are you timid and fearful, or are you prepared to take a closer look at your business, and your business goals, and make changes that seem necessary for success?

A common change made by many businesses is one of "positioning." Positioning has a lot to do with what you call yourself or your products and services, and everything to do with the prices you can command for them. Let me reemphasize what I stated in Chapter Three: *that the wrong name can automatically position you in the wrong market simply because it creates the illusion in buyers' minds that you are selling something other than what you actually offer. And, if you're selling the right thing to the wrong market—or vice versa—you may be getting only half of what your products and services are actually worth.*

If you enter the marketplace with prices that are too low to begin with, your prospective buyers and customers may think you less worthy than your competition, being naturally suspicious of anyone who would offer good products or services at such low prices. On the other hand, prices that are too high can just as easily position you in customer's minds as being totally out of their financial reach, and these may be the very people you're counting on to build your business. Thus pricing becomes an important part of your overall marketing strategy, and you can't set the right prices without a thorough understanding of your costs, your industry, the economy, and a dozen other factors, not the least of which is your reputation as a business owner, entrepreneur, expert, or whatever.

There comes a time, I've learned, when it's necessary to raise prices not merely because they are justified by increased inflation or the cost of doing business, but simply as a matter of principle. For example, through the years I've gradually raised the fee I charge for workshops, seminars and keynote addresses, not out of greed, but because the audience I'm now marketing to expects nationally-known authors like myself to charge accordingly. I would soon lose credibility as a small-business authority if I didn't.

Now relate this logic to your own business. If you do something better than someone else, don't be afraid to say so, and *charge accordingly.* Be prepared to lose a few customers and prospects when you raise your prices, but also note that you'll automatically attract a whole new audience of buyers who can now relate to you because your pricing fits their preconceived notion of what a business like yours ought to charge for its products and services. I firmly believe that, as water always seeks its own level, so too will a business find its own level (market) by the way it prices its products and services.

The Illusion of Success

While you're waiting for success to happen to you, remember

Marketing Trends

A New York marketing consultant has emphasized that comfort, convenience and indulgence are important marketing trends for the 80s and beyond.

The harder people work, the more they believe they deserve something special in return, so high on their list of treats are gourmet foods and quality merchandise of all kinds. Today's buyers are also yearning for simpler things, and are returning to traditional values.

Position your business to fill such needs, and you'll do well.

* * *

Now Here's a Positioning Statement for You!

The owner of a beauty shop doesn't just "do women's hair." No, she says, "I satisfy the need for physical enhancement among working women in my town who don't have much time."

Ask yourself what special needs your business satisfies, then create a strong positioning statement of your own.

"Star Quality"

In an interview, comedian Tim Conway once said he didn't think of himself as a "star," but that he had learned early on the importance of surrounding himself with people who were stars. He said that the very fact that he was always in their company made others think of him as a star, too.

Interesting, isn't it? It works that way in business, too. To become a professional in any endeavor, it's a good idea to surround yourself with professionals. That old saying, "You're known by the company you keep," makes a lot of sense in this light, and Conway's remarks also add weight to the illusion-of-success comments at right.

"Star art" above courtesy of Eileen MacIntosh.

the importance of maintaining the *illusion* of success, especially in those darkest hours when even you begin to have serious doubts about what you're doing. Make your business look financially successful even when it isn't by having classy letterheads, business cards, brochures, catalogs and other promotional materials. And when dealing with business contacts, always speak in confident terms.

People in the business world like to deal with confident, successful people because it makes them feel more important. And since nothing sells like success itself, even the illusion of success may be enough to convince a prospective buyer that your products or services ought to be seriously considered for purchase. Nowhere is it written that you have to be honest to the point of saying, "You're my first wholesale account," or, "I have only a few accounts right now." Instead, you might say something like, "I can't believe the response I've received." You won't be lying, but you'll certainly be giving the impression that response has been terrific. Think about it. Half of all big business is ONE BIG BLUFF, and you might as well play the game, too.

After I published the above remarks in my newsletter, a reader sent these comments in response:

"You cleared up a point I had accepted in theory—maintain the illusion of success—but which I had not really been practicing. Now I can't wait for a chance to try it out. Sometimes we have an idea firmly in mind, but ONLY in mind, and just need a comment from a different angle to see how it can really be put into practice for us."

Another reader saw it quite differently, however, saying that what I was suggesting was "borderline dishonesty." Since her business acquaintances are friends, she believes that her business relationships have to be built on trust and honor, just like her personal relationships.

It's natural for different people to have different opinions on a topic like this and, in the end, we must all do what we believe to be right for us. Since I've had many years' experience in the "hard, cold, business world," I naturally have a different attitude about business than many of my readers. Although I've always handled my business and personal relationships with integrity, I've also learned that it is NOT good business sense to tell all you know when you're negotiating a business deal or trying to close a sale. You can be honest and loyal while still "playing your hand close to your vest."

I'm reminded of a job my husband got shortly after we were married. He was a freelance drummer in Chicago at the time, and there was a great deal of competition for each job in town. When a contractor called and asked Harry if he had four tympani (kettle drums), Harry said he did. "But you don't have ONE drum, let alone four," I said worriedly. "Yeah," he replied with a grin, "But I know where to GET them. If I'd been totally honest, I'd have lost the job."

Another letter in response to my illusion-of-success-editorial came from Linda Highley, who wrote:

"My ideas for ways of using the 'illusion of success' theory all involve emphasizing what is positive about my work and ignoring the negative, unless, of course, doing

that could cause a problem for someone. I try to base my life on the Golden Rule, and I don't see any conflict with that if I tell a shop owner, 'This is my most popular item.' It doesn't matter whether you've sold three dozen or three hundred; if you've sold more of them than anything else, it's your most popular item. If the number sold is important to the buyer, he'll ask. It also sounds more positive to say, 'This is a new design,' instead of 'I haven't sold any of these yet,' though both statements are true.

"I'm sure we've all found ourselves in a strange town at meal time, and nearly all of us will choose to eat at the restaurant with the larger crowd. That's reacting to the 'illusion of success,' and if we really want to be successful, looking as if we already are is a good way to start."

Joyce Goad also wrote to share her feelings on this topic, adding weight to both my remarks and those of Linda's above:

"When I first started out with my paintings and crafts about five years ago here in Florida, I took my paintings to the first store where the owner liked my work and bought everything. Then he said he would like paintings of Florida wildlife, and could I paint pelicans especially. 'Oh, yes, of course," I said. But really, I had never painted a pelican in my life and at that point I couldn't have said if they had webbed feet or not! But if I had said no to him, I feel I wouldn't have been commissioned for wildlife paintings too."

A Scary Marketing Story

Here's a scary story about a product that didn't sell, sent by a reader whose name and location must be kept confidential. She writes:

"A friend of mine invented a board game about a city in which she lives—population three million. She then had 10,000 games produced at a cost of $37,000.

"She reasoned that in a city as large as hers, she would have no difficulty selling 10,000 games. However, after using all the media publicity available, she is left with over 9,000 unsold games and 20 very angry shareholders.

"MORAL OF STORY: Be extremely wary of producing something that can be sold only in a limited location."

Editor's note: And NEVER rely on publicity alone to sell a product or service. Careful market research and established marketing channels are essential for success in this kind of venture.

Guerrilla Marketing

In his excellent book, Guerrilla Marketing, (Houghton Mifflin Co.), Jay Conrad Levinson stresses the fact that marketing is truly a long-distance run to which you must be committed.

Levinson is a powerful writer who makes you feel good about yourself as he guides you through the marketing process. Here's a passage from the book I particularly liked:

"You evolve a marketing plan, revise it and rerevise it until it is a powerful plan for your purposes. You put it to work, and then you stay with it, no matter what. You watch it slowly take effect, rise and falter, take a bit more effort, slide back a bit, start taking hold even more, stumble, then finally grab on and soar, taking you with it. Your plan is working. Your cash register is ringing. Your bank balance is swelling. And it all happened because you were committed to your marketing program."

Levinson points out that fewer than ten percent of the new and small-business people in America have never explored all of the marketing methods available to them. Guerrilla marketing, he adds, demands that you scrutinize every single one of these methods and more, then use the combination that seems best for your business.

Tips for Success in The Plush Animal Industry

In response to the article at right, a reader sent this note:

"Dakin says it regularly sues toymakers who copy their critters. We routinely send credit checks on our gift shops to manufacturers, including Dakin. We recently received one back with our teddy bear clipped off our stationery. I suppose it was sent to their design department. And THEY talk about suing?"

Help for Product Designers

Lisa Gawne Hantzis, owner of Lisa People in San Pedro, California sent these enthusiastic comments about Inventors Workshop International Education Foundation:

"This is a nonprofit organization to which I belong and have found to be extremely beneficial to the development of my business (creator of original dolls). Those beginning nightmares of copyrights, trademarks and patents, etc. can be a confusing issue, but Inventors taught me how to do it myself, and guided me every step of the way. With the support of this organization, many 'ripoff mud-holes' can be avoided."

(Address is in the resource chapter.)

An article by staff reporter Carrie Dolan in a 1984 issue of *The Wall Street Journal* is as timely today as when first written. It stressed the fact that competition for innovative stuffed animals is ferocious.

"Trying to determine which animals will please the market is a serious matter in the $400 million plush industry," she reported, adding that the ideal stuffed animal is "soft, deliberately cute, and a threat to nobody."

R. Dakin & Co. is one of the nation's largest makers of stuffed animals. They introduce about 200 new animal designs each year, this article indicated, in an effort to keep pace with changing consumer preferences. They said "cuddliness" is what moves merchandise, and their marketing people and designers may spend months working out the details of an animal design, studying changing consumer tastes, and figuring out how to appeal to all types of people.

This article yielded a number of excellent guidelines for serious toy designers. Briefly, to sell well, stuffed animals:

● Must be appropriate to a region. (Don't try to sell pelicans to people in Detroit.)

● Must not look mean or anything like a real, dead animal.

● Should exhibit, in an endearing way, personal characteristics of buyers. (Example: Cute, pudgy animals may appeal to pudgy buyers.)

● Should have a certain look—cocky, coy, bashful, sexy, etc.

● Should have a clever name. (Example given in the article was a 1961 best seller—a turtle in a beach hat wearing a lei and named Honolulu Harry." Sold three-quarters of a million copies.)

● Should feel "plush." Said one industry executive, "Excitement of the tactile senses is the major new dimension in plush."

Also discussed in this article were the techniques used by commercial toy designers. At Dakin, for example, artists work from books filled with all kinds of eyes, noses or muzzles. They study plush materials which are laid out like samples in a carpet store. Then they begin to piece together an animal, much as one would put any puzzle together, moving eyes this way or that, changing a smile, lifting or lowering an eyebrow.

Once a design is approved, a die of the pattern is cast, and it's used like a cookie-cutter to clone thousands of animals. Most manufacturing is done in Asia.

Thus, if you are trying to compete with "the big guys" in this industry, be absolutely sure your design is original when you introduce it to the commercial marketplace. Dakin says it regularly sues toymakers who copy their critters.

PRICING TIPS FOR HOME-BUSINESS OWNERS

by Donald W. Caudill

Although both Anthony and Regina, a Virginia couple, took several marketing courses in college, they were at a loss when it came to pricing the beautiful arts and crafts they made in their home business. They knew that most of their friends involved in similar enterprises simply added their cost of materials plus a set amount per hour for labor to an ample profit margin, and magically arrived at a selling price.

This formula didn't always work. Some items sold like hotcakes, while others similarly priced were poor movers.

They consulted with a professor from the Small Business Development Center of a university, and he suggested they price their products based on a concept called "perceived value." In simple terms, this technique involves looking at the finished item (whether art, craft, or any other type product or service) and writing down the first retail price which comes to mind. It is important not to consider cost of materials or labor at this juncture; just decide the largest amount you would expect to pay. Then and only then does one calculate the cost. This amount (cost or "floor" price) is compared with the first one ("ceiling" price). If you charge below the floor price, you lose money. Charge above the ceiling price and you'll receive very few sales (if any). The *best* selling price is somewhere in the middle.

What the couple discovered startled them. They could have received at least twice the price they were charging for the "hot" products. Further, the slow-moving merchandise should have been priced less for quick sale and volume profits. When they changed their pricing strategy, they realized a substantial overall net profit increase (although on a few items, they were making only a small percent).

Here are additional practical pricing suggestions for homebased business owners:

1. Price is an indicator of quality. This means that higher-quality merchandise should be priced relatively high to attain an image of superior workmanship and value.

2. Customers have a reference price and an acceptable range. A buyer's reference price may be what your competition is charging, what he last paid, or what he feels is an appropriate or fair price. It must be remembered, however, that a buyer does not have only a single price he will pay, but rather will buy if it is within reason. If your asking price is outside of his range (either above or below), then he will not buy. While a low price would, on the surface, seem like a fantastic deal, it forces the buyer to think something may be wrong with the product.

3. Use "6," "7," and "9." Some researchers believe that there exists some magic in ending a price in six, seven or nine. Seven, as you know, is a lucky number; six and nine double and triple the powerful and mystical three. Others suggest pricing on the even dollar because buyers automatically round up to the nearest round figure.

4. Customers are influenced by your image. A homebased business that projects a professional image will always receive more business and can charge higher prices. Little things and attention to detail mean a lot and, most importantly, result in referrals.

5. Have at least a 15% reduction on sale items. Most consumers are not influenced (and, indeed, cannot perceive) a price reduction until between 12-15 percent. Therefore, a 10%-off sale usually will not attract much business. Moreover, customers expect to get a discount when purchasing multi-units. When a customer purchases two or more of your items, it is suggested you offer a discount of at least 15% after the first item.

6. Do not follow tradition. Some entrepreneurs argue that one must "go along to get along." That is, if everybody else is charging a certain amount for an item, you should follow

(continued, over)

suit. However, many successful homebased businesses have broken price barriers and demonstrated that most price traditions are invalid. Additionally, it is suggested one never get involved in a price war because both companies lose. A price war is a lose-lose situation even though you may feel you won. A much more desirable strategy is to offer to *match* or *beat* the competition's price on one item at a time.

A homebased business can easily enhance its bottom line by carefully planning and enacting a new or improved pricing strategy. Many success stories abound concerning people who did just that. While considering costs is important, one must also weigh the other equally-important variables in playing "The Price is Right!"

_____

Donald W. Caudill, Assistant Professor of Marketing at the University of North Alabama, is a consultant for scores of small and large businesses. He is also a popular speaker and seminar leader who has been published in several professional journals and trade publications.

HELP OTHERS MARKET THEIR WARES BY PUBLISHING DIRECTORIES

In 1980, Professor Jack Mandel published the first edition of his now very successful guide, *The Long Island Arts, Fine Crafts and Collectibles Directory*. As a professor of small business management and crafts marketing at Nassau Community College in Garden City, New York, Jack had a natural interest in wanting to help local artists and craftspeople connect with potential customers seeking handmade goods or services.

The idea has worked, and Jack thinks others could easily follow in his footsteps, publishing guides for buyers, sellers and suppliers in their own areas.

"It takes time to research your area, plus some sales ability, organizational skills, and a good printer," says Jack, "but I have found this to be a very lucrative opportunity."

Mandel's directory is different from other self-published books in that it contains pages of advertising, which revenue underwrites his publication cost and makes him a profit even before the directory is published. His latest edition has 220 pages and sells for $7.95. He projects next year's earnings to be $35,000—not bad, he says, for a part-time venture!

Is it difficult to get advertisers? You bet. When Jack first began, he sold only 40 out of 1,000 contacted. Now, each time he publishes a new edition, he spends more money to make it look better, which in turn encourages additional advertisers next time out.

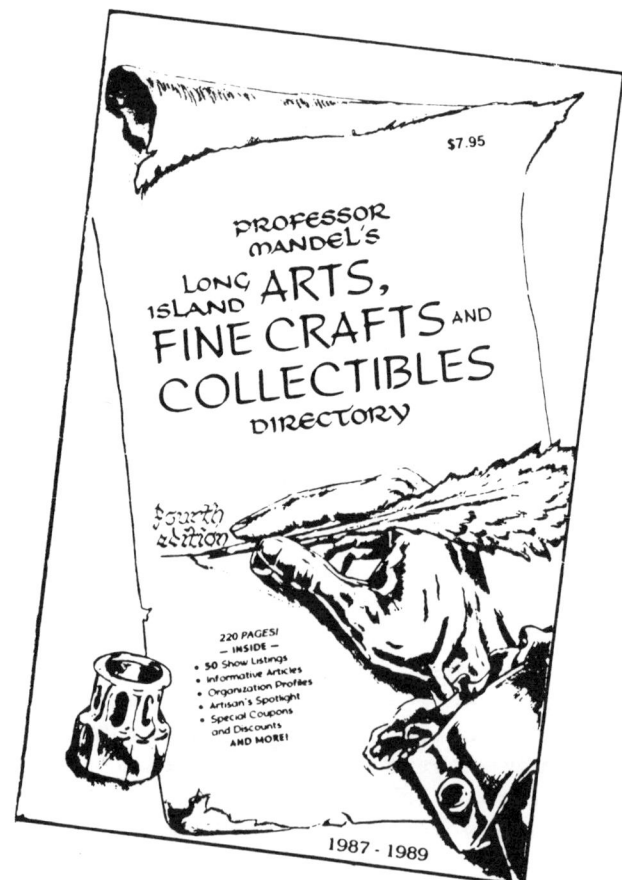

PROFESSOR MANDEL'S
LONG ISLAND ARTS, FINE CRAFTS AND COLLECTIBLES DIRECTORY

$7.95

fourth edition

220 PAGES!
— INSIDE —
• 50 Show Listings
• Informative Articles
• Organization Profiles
• Artisan's Spotlight
• Special Coupons and Discounts
AND MORE!

1987 - 1989

If you'd like to self-publish a directory in your home town, you may benefit from Professor Mandel's "Arts Self-Publishing Kit," listed in the resource directory.

SELLING TO CANADIANS

by Leila Albala

The U.S. market is vast, indeed...but have you considered Canada's 25 million customer prospects? As this writer explains, it's a market worth exploring.

You might consider the U.S. market so vast that you haven't even thought about selling to Canadians, but there are over 25 million people in Canada and their buying power is by no means small. Even if you don't actively solicit orders from Canada, you might receive them anyway. We Canadians read a vast variety of American newspapers and magazines and respond to ads for products and books not available in Canada.

Selling across the border is very easy. Usually Canadians pay in U.S. funds even if you don't specify it in your ad or order form, but many U.S. Companies stipulate "*Canadian orders, add $—, all prices in U.S. funds.*" Postal money orders or U.S. bank money orders work fine and you can also use VISA and MasterCard. The right amount is charged automatically in local currency from your client.

Personal checks work fine, too, but many companies discourage them since they may have to pay an extra dollar to deposit each check. Clearing may take a long time and it can be hard to collect if a check bounces for insufficient funds. I have, however, accepted personal checks for years from U.S. customers, since I realize they are the easiest type. I have had hardly any troubles at all, even though I don't even wait for the check to be cleared first.

There is no duty payable on books, catalogs, or brochures. Other products, such as fabrics or kits, would be subject to duty. That makes things more complicated and can discourage many would-be clients. The duty can be high, currently 25% for fabrics. That's why most American fabric clubs say, "*Sorry, no Canadian orders*" in their ads. It is not only the currently-unfavorable exchange rate for Canadian dollars, or the extra price to pay for duty; it is mainly the fact that, depending on where your client lives, she may have to go to the nearest customs office to pay and claim her package. If that office is more than 20 miles away, she will think twice about ordering across the border.*

If you wish to get orders from Canada, advertise in magazines and newspapers in the U.S. that have subscribers and newsstand readers also in Canada (check this with the magazine's circulation department).

American magazines sell in Canada often better than Canadian magazines, and are widely available. Some American companies advertise regularly in Canadian media. If you have a craft product and wish to advertise it in Canada, you might try *Hands* or *Crafts Plus* magazines, for example. *(Ed. note: See resource chapter for addresses.)* Both will yield addresses for many other Canadian publications, catalogs, stores, etc. that might be right for your products.

Even if the Canadian population is only 10% of the U.S., the response here to your product might be much greater in comparison. In several American magazines there are so many craft books and kits that your product, no matter how different, is still only one of many. When advertised in a less-crowded Canadian magazine, however, it might be the only one of its kind, and therefore be more likely noticed.

Leila Albala is the owner of ALPEL and author of several sewing pattern books which she has self-published and sold successfully (over 60,000 copies) in the U.S., Canada, and several foreign countries. In fact, she went to Finland recently to negotiate a book contract with that country's largest publishing house. "I gave lots of magazine and newspaper interviews," she said, "literally talking my books into windows in several bookstores." Another article by Leila appears later in this chapter.

_____

Books are an ideal product to sell to Canadians. *Easy to ship and unbreakable, these non-duty items are delivered right to a customer's door.*

HOW TO TAP
THE MUSEUM SHOP MARKET

─────────── *by Diane Lea Mathews* ───────────

One of the first rules in successful marketing and advertising is to determine your "target audience"—your potential buyer. Museum shops are potential customers for handmade craft items, but because there are so many diverse kinds of museums—from colonial forts to computer museums—you need to pinpoint those that are appropriate for your type of craft.

Museums must be very selective in what they offer for sale in their shops due to their educational, nonprofit status. Items must be closely related to the museum's collections and sales of unrelated items can make the museum subject to "unrelated Business Income Tax" (UBIT). This tax is imposed on the revenues from sales in a museum's shop of individual items that the IRS considers "unrelated" to the museum's educational purpose.

To determine which museums (and this includes local, county and state historical societies, zoos, botanical gardens and arboreta) are the best prospects, you can refer to *The Official Museum Directory*. (For address, see American Association of Museums (AAM) in Resource Chapter.)

A Directory of Historical Societies and Agencies is published by The American Association for State and Local History (see resource chapter for address). It may be helpful in identifying prospects. Your local museum or library should have copies you could consult.

Listings in the annual AAM directory include the following information on over 5200 museums: name, mailing address, phone, date founded, personnel (sometimes including museum shop manager's name); governing authority (municipal, individual, university, nonprofit corporation, etc.); type of museum (natural history, historic house, art, science, etc.); type of collections (antique furnishing, paleoindian artifacts, European and American paintings, etc.); facilities (library, auditorium and sometimes indicates "items for sale"); publications (their own books, newsletters); hours, admission price and cost of membership.

Of most interest to craft (and other product) sellers is type of museum and type of collections. The AAM directory has an index to institutions by category that will help determine possibilities. The next step will be to carefully read each listing to see if your type of craft may be of interest to the shop manager. Keep in mind that what the shop sells must be closely related to the collection. A museum which has a collection of bird bones and reconstructed Eocene whales will not be interested in buying dried flowers.

One way to increase the buyers' interest and to satisfy the "related" requirement is to prepare descriptive literature that tells how your particular item relates to the collection. An example of this is a simple tag that explains that your item features a design based on something from the collection (a royal scarf adapting the design from the enameled hilt of a 19th-century oriental prince's sword, a waistcoat striped tie, illustrating 18th-century fabrics, jewelry patterned after a design from a North Syrian parapet, etc.).

If your product line is suitable for a wide variety of museums, the publisher of the AAM directory (see National Register Pub. Co.) has made mailing lists available through Aggressive List Management, Inc. You can select from 13 museum categories.

Museum shops are like most other gift shops in that they want to deal with people who maintain a professional attitude. You must be willing to accept purchase orders and to sometimes submit as many as three copies of the invoice, but this extra effort can result in sales otherwise not made. And, so far, I have had no trouble over prompt payment.

──────────────────

Diane Lea Mathews has worked professionally for 10 years in the historical-museum field, and in the past few years has been selling her herb-related books to museum shops. She is now expanding sales with the addition of potpourri and sachets (made from 19th-century recipes) by using the above information to determine the best potential buyers. See resource chapter for information about Diane's Herbal Kitchen newsletter.

YOUR IDEAS MAY BE WORTH A FORTUNE!

by Woodie Hall

A good idea doesn't care who it happens to," says Woodie. When one happens to you, you should do something about it."

You cannot force ideas to happen, but you can learn the route to take from the "brainstorm" to the bank.

To succeed, you must first have a good idea. The best ideas are those that help people do something faster, better, easier or cheaper; or, if it makes people healthier, happier, stronger, sexier or richer, you will be on the right track. The greatest enemy of success is the fear of failure; don't succumb to this—you could be throwing money away.

If you are like most people, you have had several good ideas, but never did anything with them. Why? I've found there are four basic reasons why people fail to profit from their good ideas: (1) They decide their idea is absurd or foolish; (2) They feel someone else has already thought of it; (3) They don't know how to protect their idea and they have a natural rear it will be stolen; and (4) they have a total lack of marketing know-how.

I stopped giving away my ideas in 1968, and since then I have placed more than 150 product ideas with manufacturers. Most of my creations have been fun things like toys, games, puzzles, novelties, and affordable "gimmick gifts."

Basically, I market my own ideas. I don't recommend invention-marketing firms because investigations have revealed that many of these are "front-money phonies" that have been defrauding inventors. The Federal Trade Commission is concerned that the 250 major idea-promotion firms may be violating the law by promising would-be inventors to find a producer for their products.

If an idea is not complicated and is seasonal, or of a novelty nature, my book explains how to find someone to manufacture it without a patent and without the help of a lawyer. For the person who wants a copyright, patent, or trademark, my book provides guidance. It also suggests instances when the help of an attorney is needed.

There is nothing that a manufacturer would rather do than pay you a royalty for something that will make him a lot of money. Most gimmicks have about a one-year life on the novelty store shelves, but some stay popular for several years and others are reborn for the next generation of novelty fans. If you have ideas for new products, don't be bashful about trying to sell them. No matter how dumb they may seem, someone, somewhere, will be glad to use them.

Editor's note: Among the many novelty items Woodie has sold to manufacturers over the years are: a set of phony/humorous credit cards; "Kick Dice," (a pair of giant foam-rubber dice good for venting frustrations or playing pool polo); a variation of the World's Greatest series of little loving cups; Zodiac Dice; napkin designs for Bon Voyage parties; the "Golf Nut" trophy; the "Good Egg Award," and "Happy Edibles," (such as a mounted onion that says "I cry for you," and a walnut that says, "You Crack Me Up.")

For more than a decade, Woodie has been receiving publicity about his success in selling ideas. He's been a guest on 134 radio and television programs, received stories in over 2,000 newspapers, and been written about in 91 magazines. He's also given countless free lectures to a variety of audiences.

He adds: "When I retired in 1971, my hobby was marketing ideas. Now my favorite hobby is to do things that will help and encourage others to develop and market their ideas. You might say I'm in a race against time. The older I get, the more I want to do to help and encourage others. It's exciting...and I'm also wondering who will do the encouraging when I'm not around."

See the resource chapter for information on how to order Woodie's book, Your Ideas May Be Worth A Fortune.

HOW I GOT THOUSANDS OF DOLLARS' WORTH OF FREE MARKETING ADVICE

by Carl Betz

I got my free marketing advice from Wharton Business School, University of Pennsylvania, Philadelphia, by first contacting the professor of marketing with a letter outlining the business history of Glass Creations—its successes and problems with merchandising.

I listed a host of questions we were perplexed by, including packaging problems; pricing questions (were prices too high or too low?); marketing queries such as how the public perceived our glass, would they buy as a collector, or for gifts or personal use, what new models might they like, what price would they be willing to pay on a new model we just developed, and so on.

Samples of our product (see illustration this page) were also provided. The professor then presented our products and letter to his students and they then had the option to contact me if they were interested in doing their senior project of our business. This would require a survey of 50 (minimum) individuals and 15 (minimum) retailers, questionnaires, mail survey, etc. There were three men and three women all ready to graduate, applying their four years' of college learning in merchandising to our product. So, for free, I got 24 years of "smarts."

After a couple of get-togethers with the students, they evolved the questionnaires, and in about four months I had a formal presentation (with wine and cheese snacks) of their findings, which included a 150-page printed report, a two-inch-thick stack of computer statistics, six alternative options and suggestions on how to revise and improve our catalog and mailer sheets—plus a new design mailer with appropriate artwork which was to be used to broaden our sales base.

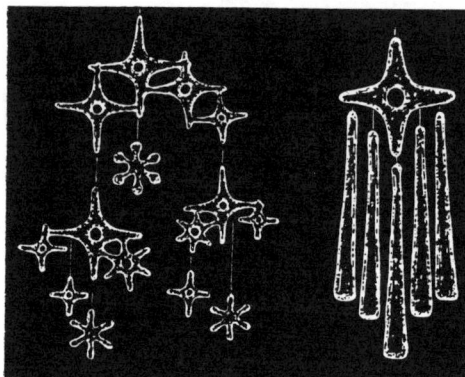

We paid only for the cost of phone calls and printing of the reports—less than $200. Their report was quite comprehensive and certainly would have cost several thousand dollars if done privately. Although much of the data they provided had been known for years, it was never digested to a point of proper interpretation and then reduced to a program for implementation.

Editor's note: Carl's experience suggests that other businesses might be able to get similar free advice from marketing classes in nearby colleges or universities. Certainly it's worth considering.

Although Carl has recently retired and is no longer producing his Glass Creations, they are still available, he informs me, "as long as inventory lasts." (Send an SASE if you want this information. Address in Resource Chapter.)

Leila Albala's NO-RISK

TEST-MARKETING METHOD

Although my no-risk test-marketing method is by no means unique, I wonder how many readers know what they can do when without money, or when in doubt about demand for a particular product.

Lacking money to publish my first book, I used this method to test the market prior to publication. Now I've used the same method five times, and it has worked every time. The good news is that it's not limited to books alone; I have also used it successfully to launch a new craft product.

First, here's my method for selling books prior to publication. Before I print the book (and even before I have completed writing it), I start sending out brochures with a special pre-publication price. Each time I've done this, the advance orders have paid the printing bill plus boosted my energy to complete the work.

In the case of my craft product, I had developed this idea of enlarging miniature patterns into full-size by means of a reusable plastic sheet with a one-inch grid printed on it. The system works well, and I describe how to make such a sheet in all my books; but I was curious to know if such a sheet would sell, and at what price. Although this time I would have been able to risk the money, I tested the sheet the same way as for my books.

First, I wrote to 50 customer prospects and asked their opinion. I got 42 replies; 37 of them said "Yes, please go ahead, I'll be your first customer." (The rest said yes, the idea is wonderful, but they already had made their own sheet as shown in my book, and wouldn't spend the money to buy one.) I asked for an honest opinion—not flattery—and let each person choose one complimentary book or product from my brochure for their time and trouble.

Then I contacted manufacturers, got prices, printed brochures (that was in March), and sent them out. The brochure combined sales information about my Halloween book, not yet written, and my enlargement sheet called *Duplicut*[R]. Each item was offered at an advance-order price of $7.95 plus $1.50 for shipping. I said the products would be available August 31 (or before), on which date the price would increase to $12.95 each. I got 784 orders for *Duplicut* and 955 for the book before that August 31 date. Advance orders were thus high enough to pay for the printing of 5,000 books and 3,000 gridded vinyl sheets. I was amazed by the demand for *Duplicut* since my readers could make this sheet themselves. But as they said, it is a lot of work to draw a perfect grid, so they are glad to pay for one.

The prepublication price was to test the demand. If there would'nt have been enough orders, or if I hadn't been able to complete the book for some reason, I simply would have returned the money saying how sorry I was. Incredibly, many people ordered as early as May and June, even though they knew they wouldn't get the merchandise before September.

In summary, I believe my no-risk, test-marketing method would work for many small business owners. For financial reasons and plain common sense, why should you invest your own money if you can get it from customers in advance to secure the manufacturing and success without risk?

Leila is the owner of ALPEL and author of several sewing pattern books which she has sold with great success in the U.S., Canada and several foreign countries.

See the Publicity Chapter for information on how the above prepublication technique enabled Leila to get more than 370 orders (with checks enclosed) from Vogue Pattern *readers.*

ADVICE FROM TWO MAIL ORDER PROS

Viv and Art Sloane owned a craft supply shop for three years. They got out of the business in late 1983 partly because of too-high overhead costs. With an established line of supplies and materials for the doll and miniature trade, it seemed natural to move their business into the home and go into mail order sales, Art says.

"We thought there would be little overhead costs and we could continue to have a small income with little work. How wrong we were," emphasized Art. Here, he talks about the business and shares knowledge based on experience.

During the summer of '84 we took a cross-country trip with catalogs, fliers and signs on our pickup. We dropped off fliers in many antique shops and doll shops, and even handed them out at rest stops upon request.

One of our best decisions concerning catalogs was to charge for them but to make a refundable offer on the customer's first order. Our first catalog, then 20 pages, cost $1.50 with that price refundable. The catalog now has 50 pages and costs $3.50, with $2.50 refundable with the first purchase. The cost has never seemed to deter a serious customer.

We started running nationwide ads in the *Doll Reader* and *Nutshell News* in August, 1984. We paid for the ad monthly, and as business improved we began to look for discounts for repeat ads. Our decision was to go for six months and it proved correct since after awhile catalog orders picked up.

We think that when an ad is repeated, people think you are a reputable firm and not just a "fly-by-night." We still receive orders for catalogs from the first ads. We now advertise in ten nationwide specialty magazines. Our customers have suggested magazines and newsletters to us, and we really appreciate it. We advertise only in classified sections and are not sure if we would do better with display.

Here are some suggestions we would like to pass on concerning our business and similar types:

● **Catalogs:** If you are doing black and white, if at all possible have your own duplicating machine. Catalogs sell your merchandise, and you can control quality. We are now on our third upgraded machine, and some of our customers tell us they think it is better than some of their magazines. We have seen sales going up with the quality of the machine.

(We used a commercial printer once, and it was a disaster as the quality was poor.)*

Upon receipt of an order, we always send an update, which in many cases brings immediate return of another order.

● **Insurance.** It took us over a year and a half to get satisfactory insurance. Our homeowner's policy would not cover our inventory, and we were not sure how they would treat liability. We kept asking and finally found an insurance broker who gave us what we needed at a reasonable price.

Once you have the insurance, records are essential if you ever need to collect. As much as possible, we keep up the inventory and it is put into a safe deposit box at the bank.

● **Bookkeeping:** Keeping a great (not good) set of books is essential. We were audited by IRS this year and it paid off. The auditor was impressed with our books and even gave us some hints we hadn't thought about.

● **Cash Flow:** Since we needed a cash flow, we went semi-wholesale. We buy wholesale and sell to those persons with a retail license, at a price between wholesale and retail. WE buy large quantities when possible and sell lace and ribbon to dressmakers and small shops in 10 to 15-yard quantities. If a store was to buy wholesale, they would not be able to have as great a variety for customers. We both win and we have a cash flow to add to our line.

Our business is still small and personal, run by Viv and I, but it is growing very fast. Viv now works more than fourteen hours a day, and I help in the business after I finish teaching. We hope the business will never grow so fast that we can't give personalized service.

Marketing by Mail

A Collection of Tips and Observations

1. **What is most likely to sell by mail?** Marketing publications say that the top ten consumer categories by dollar volume are: (1) insurance; (2) general merchandise (home furnishings, housewares, gifts); (3) magazine subscriptions; (4) books; (5) ready-to-wear clothes; (6) collectibles, (7) automobile clubs; (8) sporting goods; (9) crafts; and (10) foods (now one of the fastest-growing segments of direct marketing).

2. **Selling by mail through a catalog?** Then you're in competition with some 6500 other companies, and you're all selling to the same segment of the population. As a small homebased, mail-order seller, you'll do best if you specialize in some small area of the field that the major marketers think isn't worth their time and trouble. They're looking for millions of dollars in return, while you can probably do nicely with only thousands.

Above all, avoid renting the same commercial lists used by major seller—unless you're sure the list really IS your market—and concentrate on seeking out smaller lists from smaller companies operating in your own special field.

If you can identify between 20,000-30,000 people anywhere in the U.S. who have a unique area of interest, this is sufficient base for starting a specialty mail-order business.

● **Tip for Catalog Marketers:** If you produce a specialty mail order catalog, you know that, more than anything, you need the names of people likely to be interested in your line of products. Your own customers are apt to know who these people are, so here's an idea to try some time: Put a note in your catalog to this effect: *"Send us 10 addresses of friends who might appreciate our catalog, and deduct $2 from your order."*

3. **Basic Promotion Rules:** Don't communicate with any audience unless you can afford to repeat your presentation at least three times. When making mailings to your house list, you can mail as often as every six weeks and still pull a good order response. Why? Because the fundamental fact of mass promotion is that only a small percentage of any audience will notice even your best promotion at any given time, and only a percentage of that number will actually take action (order). Thus, by repeating your message at frequent intervals—even by mailing the same piece again—you automatically find a different percentage-of-a-percentage now ready to respond to your offer.

Concentrate on promoting to your best audience before you spend money on a second-best audience. (Your best audience, of course, is your own customer and prospect list.) How to vary repeat promotions? Try highlighting your best sellers, your newest products. Offer special "Introductory Offers," or simply send a catalog to remind everyone of your complete line. Continue to mail your in-house list as long as you continue to generate enough orders to cover your mailing costs.

And clean your list periodically to make sure your mail is being delivered. This is expensive, true; but over the long haul, mailing a large number of pieces to bad addresses is far more costly.

How to Get a Mail Order Ad Designed Free of Charge!

Want an expert to design a good display ad for you? Don't tell them I told you this...but when you send a brochure or press release to Opportunity Magazine, *chances are you'll get in return a good sales pitch from the Merchandising Director that explains how well your product will sell in this magazine. Along with the letter will come dummy art for a suggested display ad, and surprisingly good ad copy.*

The idea, of course, is that this magazine is trying to make it easy for inexperienced advertisers to get a display ad into an issue...so they simply create it for you. The Opportunity *audience includes independent salesmen, party plan operators, distributors, jobbers and sales organization executives who sell to all kinds of retail/wholesale outlets, as well as direct to homes, offices, stores and institutions.*

Maybe your product should be marketed to this audience; maybe not. But you have nothing to lose by sending your advertising material to the editor's attention. He'll be SURE to pass it on to his ad manager!

(See resource chapter for address of this magazine.)

4. Promotional Mailings Need a Cover Letter! You can send a press release in an envelope by itself, but it is unwise to send a brochure or flyer by itself because it rarely pulls a worthwhile response. Experienced direct marketers have proven over and again that the cover letter is the most essential element of any mail package. It's length isn't as important as its content, although many tests by mailers indicate that the longer the letter, the better the response. And a P.S. is the most important part of the sale letter because it is probably the next thing most prospects read after the headline.

Do cover letters have to be printed separately? No. This is the preferred way to do it, of course, with the standard mail package being a cover letter of from 1-4 pages (it's okay to print on the back of a page), plus a flyer or promotional brochure, plus an order form and reply envelope (with or without postage).

5. Tips on Using Self-Mailers. Since smaller businesses cannot always afford expensive direct mail packages, they often elect to use inexpensive self-mailers. Good self-mailers do work, but it's a challenge to create effective pieces.

Here are some basic pointers to keep in mind when you design your next piece: (1) Remember that a mail piece can land either side up...so make sure both covers carry an effective sales message; (2) Since a self-mailer has to do the job of four pieces (letter, brochure, envelope and order form), write *tight* and use copy with a proven track record; (3) Make the first page of your self-mailer a letter or memo, since sales pieces without any kind of letter rarely pull well; (4) Experiment with interesting folds that will interest the reader. It's not necessary to stick with standard formats unless print costs are prohibitive. Finally, investigate some of the commercial printers who offer unusual self-mailers. (Several are listed in the Resource Chapter of *Homemade Money.*)

(Editor's note: I have consistently pulled a 3-7 percent order response from self-mailers that include a cover letter on page one, followed by two pages of "catalog copy" with an order form (to be cut out of page three) that backs up against the address portion on the outer page, which also has a little "sell copy" on it. My brochures cost as little as 7 cents, depending on quantity. In my opinion, they're well worth trying.)

6. The Color of Printed Materials Affects Order Response, say the experts. In one test reported in a direct marketing magazine, a self-mailer was sent to 33,000 people. Half received one printed in brown on yellow textured stock; the other half got one printed in brown and gold on white-colored stock. The yellow stock mailer produced 46% more sales than the white-stock mailer.

Interestingly, other tests indicate that while the texture of the paper is important (especially to women), the weight of the paper makes little or no difference in consumer response. And, since lighter-weight papers and card stocks will save you money, consider them whenever you get a printer's estimate. (And always weigh a dummy piece in advance of printing to make sure it does not exceed the ounce-limit you've set.)

One more tip on color: If you've been printing your flyers, brochures or catalogs in blue or green ink, try red the next time. This could dramatically increase order response because red is a more powerful color which seems to motivate buyers more than any other.

7. **The Color of Your Advertising Flyer** is also important and may have a lot to do with the number of orders (or amount of business) you receive. One mailer reported in a mail-order periodical that, in one of his tests, the same good-pulling sales letter was printed on four different colored papers and mailed to a number of prospects. He found that blue letters pulled in 2%; gold letters pulled in 7%; yellow letters pulled in 9%, and green pulled in 34% of the orders. You might want to do some experimenting of your own to see if this theory holds water.

8. **Common Direct Marketing Mistakes.** An article by marketing authority Martin Gross emphasized the most common mistakes made by direct marketers. Hoping a list is up to date is one of them. "A list has to be constantly corrected in order to be meaningful," Gross said. "The only dependable list is probably a cemetery census."

Failure to have layout and copy complement each other, not asking for the order, ignoring the inquirer, testing the untestable, and blaming order results on the time of year are mistakes made even by the most diligent of marketers, Gross says.

Many mailers insist that one month is better than another for making mailings, but Gross thinks the year now "has become homogenized. You're in business all year round, and you shouldn't give up on orders because it's income tax time or vacation time. Unless you're running a beach or ski resort," he concludes, "you're not in a seasonal business."

9. **Other Opinions on When to Make Mailings.** According to an article in *DM News,* (in mid-1986) these were the best months for certain kinds of mailings: July and December for home-interest offers; December, July, June, January and February (in that order) for offers in the self-improvement category; June, April and December for offers in the educational, technical and professional area.

Naturally, these findings are based on mail volume of large companies nationwide, and are subject to change each year. Use this info only as a guideline to determine what may be your best mailing periods, and be sure to keep good records for each and every mailing you do.

10. **Marketing to Schools and Institutions.** Contrary to what is stated above, timing *is* a critical factor when marketing to institutions, reports one direct marketing newsletter. They buy on *their* schedule, not yours. The first three months are reportedly the best mailing months, and the last three months of the year are the worst mailing months for this market, the newsletter reported, adding: "There is considerable evidence that a significantly larger number of purchases result from spring mailings when expenditure commitments for the next year are wide open, than in the fall when expenditure commitments are set."

The article concluded that a spring mailing followed by a fall mailing in the same year would naturally generate more business than a spring mailing alone.

Wasted Postage

A reader warns mail-order sellers to check and double-check the weight of all standard mail packages.

Last year, writes Wanda Morris, "I put 54 cents on many packages after the postmaster weighed a sample and told me the cost. This year, when rates increased, I went to another post office and was told the same package would go for 39 cents.

"After weighing and re-weighing stacks of the same pattern, from the same printing, using the same envelopes, one-third or more will be enough lighter to use 39 cents," says Wanda, who couldn't account for this difference. All she knows is that it was a costly lesson because the post office won't refund such overpayments of postage.

One explanation for the weight difference may lie in how the printer has trimmed different stacks of printed material, as well as how much moisture the printed materials have absorbed while sitting in inventory.

FTC 30-Day Rule

Do you know that the FTC's 30-day mail order rule does not apply to telephone orders charged to a credit card? In fact, in mid-1986, the FTC was discouraging consumers from ordering by phone for this reason. Meanwhile, the direct marketing industry was pressing the FTC to amend their rule to include telephone orders.

11. How Much of Your Ad Budget Should You Spend on Direct Mail Promotions? According to the U.S. Postal Service publication, *Memo to Mailers*, 15% of all advertising dollars are spent on direct mail (which is second only to television in advertising growth). Also, one-fifth of direct mail expenditures goes toward postage.

12. Only 85% of Bulk Mail is Ever Delivered, according to one study by the postal service and three major mailers (Doubleday, the Direct Marketing Association, and *Reader's Digest*). Postal Service inspection files have revealed that more than 200 postal employees have been arrested in the past two years for stealing or dumping mail. Whether this accounts for some of the lost mail, or whether it simply disappears in the postal system is anyone's guess.

The Postal Service is trying to identify trouble spots in the distribution system, and is optimistic that they will eventually improve consistency and timeliness in the handling of bulk business mail (now the fastest-growing segment of the Postal Service's business.)

Editor's Note: Ten-day delivery of bulk mail is pure fiction; 20-day delivery is more likely and 30-day delivery is often the norm, in my experience. In some instances, my newsletter readers have reported receiving their issues as long as 45 days after they were mailed! Plan your own bulk mailings accordingly. My rule of thumb is that I start looking for orders or response about 30 days after I drop a mailing.

13. SASEs:Good Idea or Not? It's okay to ask people to send a SASE (self-addressed stamped envelope) for something you're offering free of charge, but when you ask for an SASE plus any sum of money, you could cut your total response by as much as 35%. (See *Homemade Money* for an interesting illustration of the difference this can mean to you in terms of dollars and overall sales of your product.)

14. Postage on Business Reply Mail. If you use business reply envelopes with postage-paid imprints, you may not realize that you are charged for such mail even when your customers affix a stamp to save you money. However, you can request a credit or refund on such postage by saving these envelopes and submitting them to the post office with a completed Form 3533, "Application and Voucher for Refund of Postage and Fees."

15. Overpayments of Postage. "If you don't have an electronic mailing scale, you're probably paying more postage than you have to," says Pitney Bowes, a leading mail equipment company. "If the weight indicator of a mechanical scale is on the line between one postage price and another, most people go with the higher amount to be safe. But this can mean paying as much as 30% in extra postage."

A Clever Way to Market an Expensive-to-Print Catalog

If you have created a color catalog featuring handmade gifts, you have quickly learned that you can't afford to mail it without charge to large numbers of people. Further, you know that classified ads offering gift catalogs for $2-$3 often yield disappointing numbers of customer prospects.

Here's one solution to this marketing problem. A shop owner in my area has expanded into mail order sales, using a mailer whose concept should work for any color catalog marketer. She has created a 11x17 inch piece, printed full color on the outside, black and white inside, and folded to 8-1/2 x 11 for mailing at bulk rates. A short sales message from the shopowner appears on the back cover, followed by good ad copy on the inside. One page gives a complete "Ordering Check List" of the dozens of items to be found in the catalog—listed by category and including item name, order number, price and shipping cost.

The other page includes black and white photos of two selected items, plus a mini order form and info on how to order the four products pictured in this promotional mailer (including the two items shown in color on the mailer's cover). The inside ad copy reads: *"We would like to send you our catalog for $3, or you may receive a complimentary copy with the purchase of any of the items listed below, a sampling of what awaits you when you browse through the 16 full color pages."*

This appears to be a terrific way to offset the costs of an expensive color catalog, and by getting shop visitors to sign a registry book, a good mail order list of interested buyers can be created. This colorful "mail order teaser" not only serves to advertise the catalog, but probably brings in a good number of orders on its own.

The Age of Skepticism

A new reader once wrote,"You may be a hoax and you're really a grumpy gremlin raking in money in a cave—but your publication comes across as written by a warm and caring person, so I shall picture you that way."

While this letter gave me a chuckle, it also served to remind me that we are living in what *Direct Marketing Magazine* has called "The Age of Skepticism," which is *"...the age in which nobody believes anybody, in which claims of superiority are challenged just because they're claims, in which consumers express surprise when something they buy actually performs the way it was advertised to perform."*

So how do we sell to the skeptics? First, always be sincere when promoting yourself or your product, offer many testimonials from real people who endorse and embrace what you're offering, and don't forget to play to the three great buying motivators, which are GREED, GUILT and FEAR.

In your ad or promo copy, approach GREED as "What you can get here with less effort"; GUILT as "what you'll miss if you don't respond"; and FEAR as "what may happen to you if you don't order now." I admit it is a challenge to be sincere while also being clever enough to play on people's emotions like this, but this is a knack we all must develop if we are to become successful copywriters and mail-order sellers.

THOMAS REGISTER MARKETING RESEARCH INFO

by Margaret M. Feeney

"I am presently the Maine representative for the *Thomas Register*, which is the largest and oldest industrial buying guide and catalog disbursement system for industry," writes Margaret M. Feeney. "I work as an independent contractor from my home office, and function as an advertising space salesperson and marketing consultant to industry. It was when I became a *Thomas Register* representative that I learned the details of their advertising research, shared here."

● Research shows that 43% of all catalogs sent out in answer to inquiries arrive too late to be of any use.

● Research also shows that just three weeks after the typical catalog is distributed by hand or by mail, only 20% can be found. A full 80% are discarded, misplaced, or misfiled. And even some of the 20% will be forgotten as time goes by.

● If you distribute your catalog by mail, lists are often out of date, and you usually miss many prospective customers. Some mail requests for catalogs come from "collectors" and aren't the solid potential customers you are seeking.

● Your reps, if you have any, can pass out your catalog when they are talking to prospects, but they probably see only a fraction of your potential customers. You can offer your catalog in ads and through publicity, but this is an expensive way to generate inquiries and fulfill orders.

● Your catalog is your single most important selling tool. An independent research study showed that 97.9% of buyers said manufacturer's catalogs were very important to them in their decision to buy, but that only 29.7% of these buyers could quickly find a current catalog when they needed it. While industrial manufacturers can place their catalog in *Thomas* to overcome these problems, for other types of businesses I would offer the following solutions.

One, charge a fee for your catalog to make sure you don't spend expensive postage sending it to collectors. Also, make frequent mailings of your product catalogs, using updates in the forms of memos or newsletters, perhaps, to be sure your literature is in the mind and hand of your prospect when he/she is ready to buy.

And, to make your advertising more effective, make it very distinctive or very large, or both, to create what we call "dominance"—that is, to help the customer decide that your company looks the most capable and most qualified to fulfill his/her need for your product or service. Our research indicates that dominant or largest advertiser is 40 times more likely to be selected.

The larger your ad, the more specific buying information you can include. But don't put too much in your ad; remember that "white space" is important. If you sell wholesale primarily, try to get your company listed in whatever trade magazines exist for your business, so that you will be included in their occasional directories and lists of businesses that are used for reference by potential customers.

There is so much advertising in magazines that it is a real problem for the smaller-budget company to afford and create an effective ad. I have found networking with like-minded business, publications and business people to be very cost effective. Free publicity and word-of-mouth will always be the best and cheapest forms of advertising, of course.

Editor's note: Margaret adds that readers who sell to industrial accounts might want to request a free listing form so they can be included in the Thomas Register. And don't forget that, with this directory in hand, you can locate virtually any product or service needed in your business.

WORKING WITH A SALES REP

by Edwin R. Smith

Selling your products through a sales representative can be a wonderfully profitable or dismal, money-losing experience, depending on your knowledge and approach.

To make the most of working with a rep, you must know what a rep does and does not do. *A rep's main function is to present and sell your product to potential customers.* A rep explains to these customers your sales terms, your products' merits, your shipping terms, etc.

A sales rep is *not* a debt collector, a delivery person, a product designer, or a production planner. These are all functions that you, as a manufacturer, must consider and plan for to have a successful working relationship with a sales rep. Many products can be sold by a sales rep; however, several considerations need to be made:

● **Pricing:** Is your product priced right? Have you considered all costs of production, including labor, supplies, and shipping? Sales reps work with a wholesale price. Will your potential buyers be able to mark-up your price and still have a product the consumer is going to buy?

● **Production:** Reps want to sell products in quantity, or products that have a larger price ticket. A rep will want assurance that you can fill, in a timely fashion, all orders he sends you. If you can make only a few items that retail for less than a few dollars, most reps probably will not be interested in your line.

● **Printed Materials:** Before you can begin to work with a rep, you need to be paper-ready. That means you will need pricing sheets, sales information, and a color brochure (or pictures of some type). Most reps will write orders on their own order forms. You will then transfer these orders to your own order forms. The more paper-prepared you can be in approaching a rep, the better off both of you will be.

● **Samples:** Most reps will need at least a few samples to show the type and quality of your product. Most reps do not pay for these samples unless they are very valuable. Instead, many manufacturers memo-bill their reps. This means the rep uses the sample until it is either returned or paid for by the rep.

● **Commissions:** Before approaching a rep, you must decide what amount of commission you will pay. Reps generally receive between 10 and 20 percent on gift items.

Finding a Rep

After you've made yourself and your product "rep-ready," the next step is to find a rep. First decide what market your product is best suited to. For example, would your product fit best in a gift shop, a craft shop that sells only supplies, a department store, or perhaps a mail order catalog? Each of these areas has its own reps. Generally, reps specialize in selling to one or two types of markets.

After deciding on the market(s) you'll pursue, read trade magazines in the appropriate fields. Reps often advertise for new products; they also attend trade shows in search of new lines.

Local gift shows are a good way to see reps who carry several lines. This allows you to see how your products might fit in with their overall look, and how well a rep would show your line.

A word of caution: most gift markets allow only retail buyers, so should you decide on this approach, be discreet and present yourself as a retailer.

Another way to find reps at a trade show is to approach manufacturers of noncompeting lines and ask if they know of sales reps who might sell a product like yours.

In seeking reps, be sure to ask what kind of products they sell, and what kind of shops they call on. You want a rep who sells products that are compatible — but not competitive -- with yours. Also, if a rep sells only to stores that sell gifts—and you make sweaters—you need to seek another type of rep.

One last word of caution: be sure you feel comfortable with the reps you choose. Go with your gut feelings. Fast talkers are usually just that.

Contract Negotiations

After you've found a rep, you'll need to come to some agreements. What items does the rep want you to furnish? Will he need sales brochures, samples, product information sheets? Be sure the rep knows as much about your product as possible. Any information you can furnish will help a rep in making sales.

Be sure to discuss the amount of product you will be able to produce and the amount of time it will take you to ship. (Most stores want a product in two to six weeks after an order is placed.)

One of the most important items to discuss with your rep is sales commissions—not only the percentage, but the way they will be paid. Will the rep be paid a commission monthly on any orders written that month? A monthly payment is common, but some manufacturers pay reps their commission only after the store has paid them. Remember most stores will want at least 30 days in which to pay for merchandise, so some reps will not want to sell your product if they must wait until you are paid.

Many reps will accept and begin to sell your product without a written agreement. This is a personal business decision, and you must decide if you feel more comfortable with or without a written agreement.

A word of caution given to me by one of my reps: do not continue to sell the same product at malls and craft shows once you have started wholesaling through your rep. This will quickly alienate your reps as well as many of your accounts.

In Summary

Working with a rep can be an exciting experience when the orders begin rolling in and you are able to make larger bank deposits. As you begin selling through reps, be open and flexible to changes. If a rep is not working as you wish, ask why; there may be a good reason. But if things just are not going well, remember that you're the boss, and perhaps you should look for another rep.

Finally, be sure to follow through on everything you say. Make shipments when promised; pay commissions when due. Nothing destroys a good relationship faster than not doing as promised. In the end, if you look out for your reps, they will look out for you.

Edwin Smith owns Craftsmith, Inc., which manufactures decorative magnets, small gift items and Christmas ornaments. A former art teacher, Edwin began his business in the living room where he used to make a few ornaments in his spare time for sale at weekend craft shows. Now, Craftsmith has a full-time staff of eight and 20 part-timers who work in their homes to produce a wide range of items that sell for about $5 each. Craftsmith's line is currently marketed through trade shows and ten sales reps.

Choosing a Rep

"When I was just beginning to wholesale my line of country crafts through a sales rep," a craftseller writes, "I had to choose between two reps: one already established as the top country rep at the Gift Mart in Kansas City, the other an individual with no permanent showroom who traveled the same territory, and would have my line as his only country line."

"I chose the second because we hoped he would emphasize my line and at the same time, I might be able to keep up with the orders. I think the choice was wise. In the first season, I had a steady flow of orders with a good pre-Christmas rush, and was able to keep my delivery under three weeks while still having time to learn the ins and outs of the wholesale business.

"Now my rep has his own permanent showroom at the Gift Mart and I am better equipped to handle the increase in orders. (He charges 15% commission on the wholesale price.)

MORE ABOUT SALES REPS

by Nancy M. McFayden

There are two kinds of reps—independents and those who are part of an agency. Sometimes an area grows too large for an individual rep and they hire sub-reps at a reduced commission. Primary reps get 5%; sub-reps get 10%. The general commission is 15% (lower on food items), and agencies with a permanent showroom in a gift mart may charge more.

In a permanent showroom, you are getting constant exposure, and the reps are selling you live, not just on the road but when the showroom has its Christmas and other shows year-round.

Reps vary a great deal. If they have great enthusiasm for your products, they write larger orders, as their exuberance transfers itself to the customer. If you have (as we do) products which require a bit of knowledge to sell at their best, the rep who puts forth the effort gains the largest orders.

Sometimes certain things are sold better by women than men, and vice versa. I feel many things enter into a rep's success. Naturally, if it's a person's livelihood rather than a second income, they are more conscientious and just plain dogged!

It is the wholesaler's responsibility to supply the rep with samples, catalogs and any other aids to help sell their product. We recently invested in color sheets as an additional sales aid. Usually reps do not pay for samples, so you are making an investment when you enter into a contract. You should ask a rep to supply you with references from the other accounts he or she represents, and have a business agreement (such as the sample in *Homemade Money*) before you send samples. I always state on my packing list that samples are to be returned if the business relationship ends. You must also decide how you're going to pay commissions and on what day of the month. Of course, it is important to pay promptly.

If you have a list of accounts from advertising, these should be given to the rep for follow-up. Then there is the question of "house accounts." Some reps insist on your turning them all over to them, and as time goes on and you are busier, you may be happy to do just that. In the beginning, however, most of us want to hold onto at least some accounts we've developed and perhaps have a special rapport with. My own representatives have been very nice about that.

One way to test a rep agency is to request a catalog from a line they represent and see how quickly you receive it. One agency which I felt was a top group for "country" took six weeks to send me a requested catalog. I didn't want that kind of service for my prospective customers."

*Editor's note:
The above comments were taken from one of Nancy's letters. In a follow-up phone conversation, she told me more about her business and passed along the additional tips that follow.*

(Illustration at left is from from Gingham 'n Spice's letterhead.)

Gingham 'n Spice has been in business seven years. In the beginning, Nancy created all the products and managed the business alone. She sold the first 55 stores herself, thus proving the salability of her line. After that, it was not difficult to get the interest of reps and rep agencies.

Now Nancy has the help of several others, including some full-time employees and several independent contractors who make such items as hot pads, sachets and pillows. *(Con't. over)*

"Half my helpers are friends and neighbors," she says. "I couldn't have built my business without them."

Although Gingham 'n Spice once sold retail, the company now wholesales to some 700 stores nationwide, working with about 32 reps and 5 showrooms. A $100 minimum order ($50 on reorders) keeps the line affordable to smaller, yet high-quality stores. The line itself is best described as "a country fragrance line," which includes Nancy's own formulas for perfume oils and potpourris. Fragrance and essential oils are also sold in bulk.

I asked Nancy if most of her shops paid within 30 days, and she said yes, adding, "At present, most of my sales are C.O.D. I tell my reps to keep in mind that if I don't get paid, they don't get paid."

In selecting a rep, Nancy emphasizes the importance of getting references. "Two or three aren't enough," she says. "Get at least six or seven and ask such questions as how long the business has been dealing with the rep and what volume of orders have been generated.

Most agencies carry from 9-18 lines, Nancy points out, which means that you, as a wholesaler, must make sure that your line will not compete in any way with other lines handled by a rep agency. ("Competition" relates not only to type, but price as well.)

Finally, Nancy said that she found some of her best shop customers through representation of her products in other shops. "Shopowners frequently scout other shops for interesting merchandise, which is why it's important that your products have non-removable tags or labels."

If a tag or label gives the full address, the shopowner will probably remove it; however, inclusion of your business name, city and state is not so obvious, yet will enable a prospective buyer to track you down.

The Gingham 'n Spice, Ltd. wholesale catalog is available to readers for $1.00. A bulk oil list is available for an SASE. (Address in resource chapter.)

Breaking Into the
Christian Gift Store Market

Here's a tip from someone who cracked the Christian gift store market with a line of oak bread boards printed on one side with various Christian sayings. Says Carol Saathoff, owner of Creative Critters in Post Falls, Idaho:

"We found our rep through our contact with the manager of a large chain of Christian gift stores in this area. He told me that the Christian market is often overlooked by sellers, and it's hurting for new gift items. Forget plaques, however; there is an abundance of those.

"You definitely need a Christian-oriented rep to sell to this market," Carol adds. She was told that buyers are hesitant to buy from reps that are not familiar with this market.

Exhibiting in Trade Shows

In later correspondence with Carol, she reported on the Gourmet Products Show in San Francisco. While it did not generate the orders she had hoped for, there were other benefits. Her "Kookie Kutter Keeper" bag was noticed by Gifts & Decorative Accessories magazine and featured in an issue shortly thereafter. New sales rep contacts were made, and two new rep organizations signed. "New business friends were also made," says Carol.
"There is a special camaraderie that exists during a trade show."

A trade show tip from Carol: If you study beforehand the union regulations pertaining to the setup of booths, you may be able to avoid hiring union labor at hourly rates of $65 and up. "Our booth was constructed in such a way that union labor wasn't necessary," says Carol. "Even so, we were carefully watched during setup, and hassled a bit. However, we knew the regulations, and stood our ground."

Marketing Miscellany

● **How much should you spend on Promotion and marketing?** Here's one formula, developed by the National Association of Retail Dealers: Figure your gross profit margin (subtract cost of goods from gross sales, then translate that dollar amount into a percentage figure). Then divide this percentage figure in half. The rule is that all ad and operations costs (including salespeople) should not exceed this figure, or one-half the gross operating margin.

● **What percentage of your marketing budget should be reserved for the production of marketing materials?** About 10%," says Jay Conrad Levinson, author of *Guerrilla Marketing*.

● **New customers are costly to obtain.** Marketing studies have revealed that it costs the average company six times as much to get an order from a new customer as it does to get the same order from an existing customer. And, since your existing customers are your most profitable source of new orders, it pays to go out of your way to keep them happy — with good service, special attention to order inquiries, special money-saving offers, and so on.

● **A few words about the competition, from author Herman Holtz:** "...some entrepreneurs believe that all competition is harmful to them. But there are others who believe that competition is the best thing that can happen to them because the combined effect of everyone's advertising and sales promotion creates a much larger market than anyone can create through his or her own efforts alone." (From Persuasive Writing, published by McGraw-Hill.)

● **A good customer-feedback idea.** *NHBR* once received a letter from an office supplier who wanted to know why additional orders had not been placed after the first order a few months earlier. The letter, however, was typed only on the left-half of the page, and it began: "This half is ours. We haven't heard from you," etc. "Losing a good customer is like losing a good friend. I can't let either drift away in silence." More copy, then: "Whatever the reason, I do care. The other side of this 'half letter' is yours. I'd consider it a personal favor if you'd use it."
Write your own copy and try this idea if you want to know what's happened to old customers or clients on your mailing list.

● **Drumming up prospects.** Ruth Rhodie, of Geraldine Designs, offers this suggestion, which has worked for her in locating customers in far away and remote areas: "Whenever a friend or relative goes on a business trip or vacation, I ask if they will copy the yarn and needlework sections of the yellow pages of the phone books in every city they visit. When they return with the information, I follow it up with a call or a letter and catalog."

Selling Greeting Cards And Paper Products

Perhaps 80% of all greeting cards sold in the U.S. are produced by Hallmark or American Greetings, the two larger companies in this field. However, these companies buy little, if any, work from freelancers. To sell to the remaining companies requires research and professionalism. You'll find perspective and useful marketing tips in Designing Greeting Cards and Paper Products, *by Ron Lister. (Prentice Hall/Spectrum, 1984.) Available in Libraries.*

Booming Bridal Business

A 1986 issue of Sew Business *emphasized that cost is not the major consideration when it comes to the bridal market; people spend what they can. A research agency says over two million more marriages will take place in the 80s as compared to the 70s.*

Publicity Pays 7.

The publicity story of 1985 may well have been Canfield's *Diet Chocolate Fudge Soda.* A chance mention of this drink by Bob Greene, a Chicago-based syndicated columnist, triggered a nationwide rush on this product and absolutely boggled the minds of sales execs at Canfield's.

Green simply said that the cola helped him lose weight because it satisfied his craving for chocolate. Talk about emphasizing the benefit of a product!

Immediately afterwards, the company began to receive inquiries from dealers in more than 20 states, and consumer demand for the product caused the company to gear-up their production line for around-the-clock operation.

This product, which was not new, sold about a million cans the year before. As a result of Greene's tiny mention, however, sales the first month after this publicity were twice that amount, and year-end sales were phenomenal. Company officials who were interviewed on Chicago television stations were shaking their heads in disbelief. "I've heard about the power of the press," one of them said, "but I've never seen anything like this." Green was also amazed by the response to his casual mention of a product he wasn't even trying to promote. (No doubt he was also pleased to know how many people read and respond to his column.)

This kind of nationwide publicity may be available to you, too, depending on what you're promoting or selling. (An annual directory of syndicated columnists is published by Public Relations Publishing Co. and may be available in your library.) After using one of these directories to compile a publicity list for my books, and sending a press package accordingly, I received mentions in several columns. While none brought the kind of response mentioned above, I believe all of it together has had considerable impact on sales of my books in bookstores.

After you've located all the columnists everywhere who are writing about your special area of interest, continue to build your press release list by exploring the other publicity options mentioned in this chapter and in the publicity chapter of *Homemade Money*, which includes sample press releases and a lot of insider-secrets.

Newspapers, Radio and Television Publicity

For starters, be sure let your local newspaper, radio and television stations know what you're doing. They may be delighted to do a story about your business. Take Mary Hansen, for example, a self-publisher in Canada. She wrote a couple of years ago to tell me how much she had profited from the advice in *Homemade Money* when she began to earnestly promote her book, *Joyful Learning—Learning Games for Children Ages 4 to 12.*

"Montreal, Calgary, and Regina have done articles which have resulted in many orders," she wrote, "and best of all, the CP wire service (which goes across Canada) picked up my story, including my address and how-to-order information. In three weeks alone, I received over 1400 orders for the book! And, as you say, publicity generates even more publicity. I've recently been on local television and radio, and some stations plan to interview me long distance." Since writing that letter, Mary Hansen has continued to benefit from publicity.

A later note from Mary included this gem of PR wisdom: "I was interviewed for 15 minutes on Toronto's second largest radio station (huge numbers of adult listeners), and although my name and address was given twice, I got just three book orders from that show. On the other hand, I was interviewed for about four minutes by a much smaller station (a more intellectual, classical type of station than the other one), and I received 47 orders from that. Obviously, listeners on the smaller show were the ones most interested in kid's educational products. Just shows you the importance of 'target marketing.'"

Although publicity opportunities are unlimited, they are also fleeting at times, and must be seized quickly before the time for publicity is past. For example, dollmaker Laurie Carlson in Deary, Idaho had her dolls featured on national television during a presidential election, because, she said, some innate sense of the value of publicity prompted her to send caricatures of Reagan and Mondale to Willard Scott, who does announcements of local celebrations and the national weather scene. This action immediately brought a 4:30 a.m. call from an NBC researcher who wanted to know if Laurie had actually made the dolls. When she said yes, she was told they would be featured on that morning's telecast to "show the station's impartiality on election day." Can you imagine Laurie's excitement? I'll bet the townspeople of Deary were excited, too, to have their town publicized in this way.

Timing is also important when mailing regular press releases, as Mary Hansen will confirm. She first mailed press releases on the above-mentioned book in June, with no response at all. However, when she remailed them again in September, (back-to-school month), the media picked up on her story.

Publicity in National Magazines

Publicity in a national consumer magazine is the dream of many small business owners who have mail order products, and it may not be as hard to get as you think. All it really takes is a "reader's eye" and some common sense about what magazines are interested in writing about. Take *Family Circle*, for instance. This magazine has often featured creative individuals with unusual

Finding a News Peg

Whenever you can tie your products or services to a topic of great interest to many, you increase your chances for publicity.

In Chase's Annual Events, a directory of special days, weeks and months, you'll find more than 5,000 special events listed, including "National Anti-Boredom Day," "Swap Ideas Day," "Be Late for Something" day, and a host of anniversaries, national and ethnic days, festivals, fairs, presidential proclamations, and commercially-sponsored promotional events. (Published by Contemporary Books; available in bookstores.)

● *You might promote your handmade items during "National Home Improvement Month." What better way to "improve" one's home than to beautify it with handcrafts?*

● *There's also "Michigan Week" in May, and what better time to teach Michigan citizens more about the state, such as the many talented artists and craftsmen it has.*

● *If you have a business related in any way to pets, you can profit during "Pets Are Wonderful Month."*

● *Child-related businesses can tie into "Week of the Young Child" in April while photographers can "snap to it" during "National Photo Week" in May.*

● *The first full week in May each year is "National Small Business Week," sponsored by the SBA. This is always a good time to send a press release about your business.*

Joellen Buzinec wrote to remind NHBR readers that donations of their goods for worthwhile causes can often lead to sales. She explains:

"One of our local elementary schools has a fundraising drive each year with a variety of ways to gain extra revenue for special projects. My homebased business, JOBEE, is making children's jogging suits and personalized towels for children, so naturally I donate several of these items. The return on this investment is always many times over.

"For example, a donated towel worth $12.99 landed me a $4,200 sewing contract for a group of barbershop singers. The father of the child who won the towel started reading my brochure, and as a result called and asked me to bid on the job."

You Never Know Till You Ask

Writes Sheri Wood: "I asked the local Historical Society if they would be interested in having me demonstrate quilting for them sometime, and I now have a paid job working on special events and regularly on weekends, which opens up a lot of idea. I also got a nice article in the local paper when I finally sent out my first press release.

products, publications or services, sometimes bringing them as many as 10,000 orders or requests for additional information. These lucky individuals usually got this fabulous publicity by sending an interesting package of information to the magazine at the right moment. (My own *Family Circle* story appears in *Homemade Money*.)

In late 1985, Marion Boyer and Jo Mucha, owners of Village Vendor, Ltd. in Portage, Michigan, told me their publicity story. Their booklet, *Marketing Crafts Through a Home Party System*, was mentioned in *Family Circle* in April. As of mid-June, they had received about 1700 orders for this booklet, with 20-30 orders still coming in weekly.

"In all, this article has been a tremendous experience for us," Marion said. "It's amazing how such a mention can give a business sudden credibility! We have received countless telephone calls and letters of inquiry beyond the orders, and it's extremely exciting to find a common bond with so many people. We would encourage most anyone in business to try to think of an angle that may be worth of some publicity. If we can do it, so can they, and you never know when your efforts may pay off. Don't be afraid to go for it!"

That "angle" Marion mentioned is important. Another name for it is a "news hook." You may have the right product, but be promoting it with the wrong "hook." Again, Mary Hansen offers a good illustration: "Before, I was calling my book a 'fun way to learn,' which did not work at all in getting publicity. But when I decided to be totally direct and say that my book was a method of helping kids who were underachieving, who had not succeeded before, the media leaped upon my story! Before, I was afraid that parents would shy away from this idea because they don't want to admit that their kids are under-achievers. But I was wrong. They like my fun, humour-filled approach to teaching such children."

Where else should you look for national visibility? Publicity may await you on the "letters page" of consumer and business magazines and newspapers. These publications often print questions from readers which are a direct invitation to other readers to provide answers. If your answer happens to include a mention of some helpful product or service you just happen to offer, you'll probably find your name and address listed along with complete how-to-order information. All you have to do is diligently read the periodicals in your field to find these golden opportunities.

Janet Brewer, who formed a crafts cooperative in 1980 and now publishes show calendars, said the best piece of publicity she ever got came from a mention in *The Boston Globe*, which has a section called 'Ask The Globe.' "People write in to ask questions which the paper answers," Janet wrote. " Someone, bless her soul, wrote to ask about a crafts group in the Wilmington area that lists craft shows, and *The Globe* gave our name and address. We received hundreds of letters for weeks afterwards. Our membership doubled and we began a *Patrons of the Arts Calendar* as a direct result of this unsolicited advertising. (It makes me want to write in again someday and ask the same question.)"

And why not? I know more than one savvy promoter who's gotten excellent publicity this way.

HOW TO PROFIT FROM A MEDIA INTERVIEW

by Kate Kelly

The foregoing tips were digested from The Publicity Manual *by Kate Kelly, and reprinted by permission. Kate is a member of the American Society of Journalists and Authors. Her book provides complete information and examples on how to get free publicity without hiring a professional.*

Getting publicity about your products and services is a key element in any competitive business plan. Nowhere can that be more potentially profitable than with homebased businesses. Publicity is, in effect, free editorial mention, and it can be priceless—primarily because of the credibility it has and the awareness and image it projects.

The media—newspapers, magazines, radio and television—are always looking for new stories. Most of these stories are the result of media interviews; whether in person or on the phone, that's the way the press learns about you and your business. Forethought and planning for a meeting with the press are keys to assuring that the interview will benefit both you and your business.

Most every type of interview can be a success if you are prepared. Think about what might be discussed, what you'd like to say, and how you choose to handle questions.

Ten Tips for Success

1. Know the publication or program. See it if you're unfamiliar with it. What can you find out about the interviewer—any specialty? Does he/she know about your field?

2. Find out the context of the interview. What kind of piece will it be? Single interview? Business round-up? This will help you frame your remarks.

3. Consider the audience and speak to their interests. What information would they want to know about your business.

4. Be direct, concise, clear. Talk for copy. The reporter is writing down what you say. Make your points and stop. Don't ramble.

5. Identify your key points and stress them. Look for opportunities to do so. You can often turn a question into the chance to make a positive statement by redirecting it to your main point.

6. Avoid using "jargon." Many of your everyday business phrases can seem like a foreign language to a reporter (and your audience).

7. Ask for clarification of any questions you don't understand. It's better than running the risk of being misquoted. Clarify any statement you think they don't understand—you're often educating the press about something new.

8. You're in charge. You control the information flow, and you need not provide every detail on every subject (especially if it would reveal competitive business information).

9. Summarize your points. Be sure to recap your main points at the end of the interview. The last things you say are generally the last things the reporter writes down and remembers. Develop an answer for "Is there anything else you'd like to add?" This is a golden opportunity to restate your most important message.

10. Don't forget to give "contact" information! Homebased business owners need to stress how they can be contacted for their products or services. Be sure the reporter has your correct address and phone number.

"I just had the reception for my first photography exhibit," wrote Carol Rae Mowery in mid-1985. "The University where my work is displayed said I should try to do my own publicity because I might get better coverage if it came directly from me instead of the University's press office.

"I used the guidelines in Homemade Money to help me write it, and both of our local papers printed it. One even printed it in two parts on separate days, giving me more publicity.

"I don't know how profitable my show will be, but it certainly has let everyone know that what I do is more than a passing hobby. I was scared to make the commitment and sign the contract with the university, and as my business is very young, I was afraid to spend the money required. But I decided to take the chance. I'm glad I did because many more people are now aware of my work."

"Since the article about my photo show appeared in NHBR, I have had another show at a hospital in my area where I sold several photos and received more publicity. I wrote to the hospital art director, and she already had me on her list of people to contact for future displays because of the articles she had read about me.

"I was also contacted by an area newspaper to serve as a judge for the local part of the Kodak (KINSA) photography contest because of the press releases they had printed.

(continued next page)

Something I should emphasize at this point is the fact that while you may think your press releases have landed on deaf ears, they may actually be sitting in someone's reference file folder awaiting the right opportunity for use. As a periodical publisher, I know from experience why press releases are not always used at once. Some of those I receive may end up in my newsletter file, while others are tossed in my Crafts column folder; still others may be stuck in a file drawer, awaiting the start of some future writing project. (I might add that some of the most satisfying publicity I've received has been from writer friends who went on to write business articles or books and profiled me somewhere along the line. In 1985 alone, I was quoted in three small business books simply because I'd made it a point to get acquainted with their authors months earlier.)

The fact that The Globe kept Janet Brewer's earlier press release emphasizes the importance of regular mailings to a key contact list. You just never know when one of them will take hold. Press releases I mailed to newspapers a year ago are still generating publicity across the country, perhaps because instead of indicating "For immediate release," I used the line, "Use at will," which suggests copy will be timely for a long while. Many editors obviously held my release with the idea of using it when they had extra space to fill. I know these press releases are working because I always give my releases a special coded address. In addition, readers often send me a clipping when they ask for my free brochure.

In building your media mail list, you might think that small publications or little-known writers are hardly worth the bother when it's national visibility you're after. But don't underestimate writers—they can strike it big when least expected. And the press can be powerful, even when a publication has a limited circulation. What counts is the quality of the readership. Take my periodical, for instance. It's paid circulation has never been much over 2,000 because so many people come and go in the home-business field. But I do have a faithful core of readers who are enormously responsive to what they read in NHBR. Many people have told me about the amazing response they've received after being mentioned editorially in an issue. My readership also includes many of the "movers and shakers" in the home-business industry who read NHBR simply to connect with interesting people in this field.

For example, Susan Winchester wrote awhile back to tell me that a reporter from The Wall Street Journal had interviewed her for his column after reading about her Sweeter Measures business in NHBR. "Not only that," said Susan, "but The Omaha World Herald picked it up from there and put us on the front page of the Sunday edition with a color picture! We have had great response to our write-ups in the local papers, even though the majority of our customers are not from Nebraska. But the most amazing thing is that people are so impressed by the fact that we have been featured in the local paper. I cannot believe how easy it was to get the publicity...all I had to do was ask. Now we are working on magazines." (Susan's company makes mail order garments for tall and large women.)

And Edwin Smith, who wrote one of the articles on sales reps in the preceding chapter, sent me a clipping of the article his business received in USA Today, "...a direct result of being a part of your network," he told me. He's right. Dennis Blank, the freelance writer who wrote the article, happens to be one of my regular readers. (He's given me some good publicity, too.)

As a publicity hound who has literally built her business through mentions in magazines and newspapers both large and small, I can tell you that it's not just the big mentions that are important, but the sum total of all the visibility you get through the years. It's like the expensive "image advertising" major corporations place on television to get consumers to buy their products. While people do not always respond to publicity in a direct manner, but they often remember it later when they come face to face with your product or service business. I can recall many letters accompanying book orders which said, to the effect, "I've been reading about you everywhere."

Who's Who Directories

This is not for everyone, but I want to take a moment to comment on the many "Who's Who" directories in print today, many of which reside in libraries and are occasionally used by researchers who are looking for authorities in a certain field of endeavor. Being listed is no big deal, of course, but it is curious how many business people use mentions of such listings in their biographical material and press releases. It seems to impress the average person and may actually be helpful in increasing one's standing/visibility in their field. So if you're a leader/decision-maker/innovator in any field (to quote the Who's Who brochure), send for information on how you can be listed in one or more of the many directories published by Marquis Who's Who (listed in the resource chapter).

Since mailing the first application, I've been bombarded with invitations to be listed in every Who's Who directory imaginable and I am, in fact, listed in several—including *Who's Who of American Women*, *Who's Who in the Midwest*, and *Who's Who in U.S. Writers, Editors & Poets*. I returned the application forms for these three because they sounded interesting and, more important, because a listing was free. To my knowledge, however, no one has ever contacted me as a result of these listing.

Actually, as I see it, this is a giant publishing industry that profits from the size of people's egos. Listing in any directory is free (and I doubt that anyone is ever denied a listing if they have any credentials at all) but listees are then "given the chance" to buy a directory for their own use—at considerable expense, I might add. I haven't fallen for this trap, but I figure it doesn't hurt to have my name in print any time I can get it there for nothing. You should do the same. That's what publicity is all about.

"I have conducted photo classes at our YMCA two times now and am scheduled to be an instructor for an adult learning class at a local community college.

"For me the idea of building on each piece of publicity has been the most valuable. You never know who will read about you or where it will lead. As you can see, many of the things I have done can be traced back to that original press release about my first photography show."

Radio Publicity— As Near As Your Telephone

Stations throughout the country are interested in interviewing interesting people on the telephone, especially when their message can benefit the station's listeners.

Contact the producers of shows in your area to explore the possibilities. If you have good luck with them, expand by contacting other stations across the country.

You'll find a listing of them in the Literary Marketplace *directory*, found in libraries, and media lists of radio stations can also be purchased from several sources. Also in libraries, look for the annual media directories published by Larimi Communications, including Radio Contacts and Television Contacts.

IT'S THE ANGLE
THAT SELLS YOUR STORY

—— *by Nancy Smeltzer* ——

How do you get an editor to pay attention to you? There are lots of books that tell you how to write a press release, but there are lots of us fiber artists clamoring for attention. Some publications have hundreds of releases cross an editor's desk each day, so I've found that the trick is to make the title interesting, intriguing, and still tell the truth.

For general releases that are directed to a large number of people and publications, I don't really tailor the headline to any specific audience. It's hard enough to send out press releases to several hundred places without thinking up individual angles for each editor. This individual release technique is what I'm going to work on in the future. However, for these general releases, what I try to do is think up the cleverest way possible to tell my story in one sentence.

Pretend that you've been given one chance to say a sentence to get someone's attention before he/she goes on to the next person. What would you say to get that person to ask you more questions?

One of my first efforts at a press release had the title of "Local Science Teacher Coordinates Crafts Exhibition for the Baltimore Museum of Art." This release was about a small fibers show I did for a local museum; a feat that was not particularly noteworthy. The fact that I also teach Science was what made the story interesting, and several publications, such as *Baltimore Magazine* and *The Crafts Report* picked up on that angle.

Another unusual title of which I'm proud was "'Playing Dress-up' Grown-up Style in Wearable Art for Life's Private Ceremonies." While the wording of that title is a bit awkward to read, it certainly makes you wonder about the kind of ceremonies this artist is up to. This title helped me to get the job of writing a story about my ethnic-looking wearable art.

Another good one was "Fiber Artist, Nancy Smeltzer, Has Work Accepted Into International Quilt Exhibit." The fact that the show had artists from all over made the story more interesting than just the fact that I was in it. I'm still getting responses from that release, notably from *Quilter's Newsletter* and *Patchwork Patter* (National Quilting Association).

Sending out a release not only tells people about the immediate event, but has the added benefit of establishing you as an authority on a particular subject in the eyes of the media. For this reason, I got an interview on a local television station, because the producer had seen a photograph about one of my pieces. So, while I know that I'm missing a lot of deadlines for some publications, I'm hoping that I'm being remembered favor-ably for a later date. It takes many releases to gain name recognition, so I try to send releases every six weeks.

Remember to try to think about the most interesting aspect of your story, and use it for your next heading. For more complete information on how to write a press release, the book I've found to be the most useful is Kate Kelly's *The Publicity Manual*.

———————

Nancy, who has undergraduate degrees in studio art and biology, regularly expounds on the state of her art to anyone who will listen.

Nancy says the best compliment she has received was given to her by someone in her community who, upon meeting her for the first time, said that he had been hearing a lot about her, but thought she would be much older, considering all the publicity she had been getting.

As Nancy's visibility has grown as a quiltmaker, so have her talents as a freelance writer. She has published a series of magazine articles on how to market quilts through galleries, and often shares publicity tips in crafts and home-business publications.

Publicity Endnote

Since writing the preceding article for *National Home Business Report*, Nancy has been featured in countless publications. I chuckle every time she sends a new release and copies of the various clippings she's gotten. Clearly, she's a savvy promoter you can learn a lot from.

My favorite release of all was the one titled "Fiber Artist, Nancy Smeltzer, Quilts Her Cast As She Recovers From Hand Surgery." Even when she's unable to work, she's getting publicity! The release was accompanied by a photo of Nancy contemplating her quilted cast, which was included in *The Crafts Report* along with her article, "How to Use Press Releases to Get Yourself Noticed." Said Nancy, "I thought the quilted cast would be a good angle since carpel tunnel syndrome is in the news a lot."

When I contacted Nancy for permission to reprint her *NHBR* article in this book, she naturally included one of her latest releases, titled "Fiber Artist Has Work Accepted in Exhibit on Celestial Art," and attached several clippings of publicity given to her series of "Star Map" quilts, which naturally included "Halley's Comet," a quilting project created to coincide with the national publicity being given to this rare event. Said Nancy in December, 1986, "The publicity from the Halley's Comet release has spread out over a year. I'm still getting feedback from it."

A comment in one of those articles nicely sums up both Nancy's quilting and PR strategy: "In her classroom, Maryland science teacher Nancy Smeltzer sticks to the facts; outside, she lets her imagination soar to the heavens." If she ever gets tired of quilting, she has a great future as a publicist for new business owners!

By the way, Nancy's Comet quilt is a good example of how any enterprising business can profitably tie it's own publicity into a major media event. (For more ideas, see sidebar material in this chapter titled "Finding a News Peg.")

Leila Albala's Publicity Secrets

You'll recall Leila Albala's articles in the marketing chapter. Let me mention here that her no-risk test-marketing system also helped her get additional publicity. Vogue magazine had originally featured one of her books without giving a price. "From my previous experience," said Leila, "I knew that hundreds would write for a brochure, and that's twice the work and half the money. So I simply extended my prepublication price to their readers, and that did the trick. In the first two weeks of response, I received more then 370 orders with checks from Vogue readers—more than the total amount of orders received from a similar write-up the year before."

Leila has a knack for capitalizing on the publicity she gets. For example, when UNICEF bought ten of her Halloween costume books on consignment for their boutique in Calgary, Leila followed up by contacting their local paper, which ran an article that mentioned the fact that UNICEF was carrying her books. More than 400 books were sold by UNICEF in just two days. "They had to take waiting lists and ordered the books by courier," Leila wrote.

The second in a series of five "Star Maps" designed and quilted by Nancy Smeltzer.

On "Name Recognition"

"Products can be sold in many ways, but the only effective way to market a service is through publicity," says Dennis Hensley, author of several books, including Become Famous, Then Rich.

"Name recognition is a must in any business," he adds. "Whether you are marketing a box of cereal, an automobile or yourself, no one is going to know you exist if they do not know your name. Personal publicity and individualized public relations efforts are as vital a part of your overall business strategy as our accounts receivable, tax shelters and seminars."

Dennis is a featured author in Homemade Money, *and you'll also find other words of wisdom from him in the next chapter. His books on time management and "positive workaholism" (a phrase he coined), are especially inspiring.*

A Successful Press Kit

Writes Leila Albala: "My press kit for Easy Halloween Costumes for Children included a press release, bio, catchy covering letter, photographs, copies of previous articles featuring my books, and the book itself—all included in an orange folder with pocket. Glued to the cover was a color snapshot of Halloween costumes.

"Previously, I had just sent my book with a simple letter to magazines and, although I got write-ups in Family Circle and Vogue, most magazines didn't pick up on it. This time was different. I glued myself to the telephone since it didn't stop ringing. Editors told me they were impressed with my press kit. I was featured in ALL major Canadian newspapers, and also by the Chicago Sun-Times and the Houston Post. Leader Post in Regina gave me a whole page in color.

"Then I was featured by CBC Newswatch on Halloween night. Our local paper, Montreal Gazette, ran a small story which was noticed by an editor of a large French-Canadian magazine. She called to inquire about featuring me and my book the following year for their Halloween issue. (This is a perfect reason to translate the book in French.)"

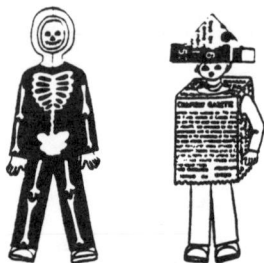

(Illustrations by Leila Albala. Copyright by ALPEL.)

The newspaper articles in total created a demand for this book in libraries, too, many of them ordering three copies to meet the demand. Months after Halloween, libraries continued to order.

See left for information on the press kit Leila used with such great success.

The Unabashed Self-Promoter

In closing, let me share some of Jeffrey Lant's philosophy about publicity. The author of several books, including The Unabashed Self-Promoter's Guide, Lant operates on the principle that all "unabashed self-promoters of worth possess information, a product or service, which will enrich the lives of large numbers of individuals. These individuals are entitled to the information we have, the media has an obligation to publicize it, and we, unabashed self-promoters, have a responsibility to insure the widest possible dissemination of information about our beneficial product or service. We also have a responsibility to build our own reputations so that we can gain even more media access and so help still more people."

I share Lant's philosophy and heartily recommend this book. You could read a dozen guides on how to get publicity, and still find reams of new information and inspiration in this one simply because Lant writes from a different viewpoint than most small business authors, thus has much to say that's new and refreshing.

The sustaining qualities of the unabashed self-promoter, he maintains, are: self-motivation, self-love, determination, and enthusiasm. If you don't have these traits, you must vow to give them to yourself now...before you have success, before you are celebrated by the media...while your cash reserves are low, and while you are still working on the development of your image and perfecting your writing style. "In short," says Lant, " before you have anything on which to base your decision except for that unfathomable gleam of inner direction, that is the moment to assume the outlook of a winner and a winner's commitment, dedication, and happy certainty about the inevitability of the desired outcome. And that moment is now."

Although Lant guarantees the methods which appear in his book, he doesn't guarantee the reader's ability to implement them. Some readers, he says, will fail to adopt the right winning attitude, some will be technically incompetent, and still others will just give up. "But for the others, a luminous future beckons," says Lant. "In this future there is wealth, the thrill of having your ideas mouthed by others, the satisfaction of disseminating your product and service to the farthest possible extent, the joy of becoming a personage, the real comfort of self-realization. These are trophies which elude most people, but they come to us, unabashed self-promoters all, as a matter of course. They are the necessary and inevitable fruits of the system laid out in the pages of my book."

Staying Motivated

8.

If you've read all the business information in the foregoing chapters, you're probably ready for some light-hearted reading at this point. I hope this chapter, based on some of my editorials in *NHBR*, will give you a few chuckles and some good ideas on how to stay motivated as you continue to develop your homebased business.

The mail I receive from my newsletter readers tells me that a lot of people are working HARD to turn dreams into reality. And they're succeeding, too. But a price is being paid for this success, and sometimes it gets a little heavy to bear. That's why, when you work at home, it's so important to connect yourself to others who share your interests, problems, and concerns. This can be done by joining your local small business network (or starting such a network if one does not exist in your area), by attending home-business workshops or small business conferences, and by communicating with homebased business owners by mail or by phone whenever an opportunity presents itself. Nothing serves as a greater motivational tool, in my opinion, than being able to discuss your small business problems with others who offer under-standing and guidance.

My periodical serves as an important networking tool in that every issue of *NHBR* includes the names and addresses of about 50 individuals, businesses, organizations, publishers, and other business connections. And every issue also includes the newest information resources I've uncovered through my own business network. Rarely does a week go by without my receiving several thank-you notes from readers who have benefited from particular information in my newsletter or one of my books.

One reason all my books have special resource chapters is because I know from experience how a single resource—just the right connection to the right person at the right time—can change the course of one's business. Take the letter I received this week from a *Homemade Money* reader. She was at her wit's end, unable to expand her present business because she couldn't figure out how to sell to the federal government, and then she found a book in the resource chapter which was the answer to her prayer. When she couldn't find the book in her library, she contacted the author who offered this book by mail and also sent her a warm, informative, three-page letter that, as she put it, was full of helpful, useful information and personal encouragement. "Let me tell you, this man made my day!," she told me in a thank-you letter. "It is nice to feel I have a future again."

> *"Refuse right now to believe there are things you cannot do. Some of the greatest things in the world have been accomplished by men and women who never knew what they couldn't do. So, not knowing, they just went right ahead and did it."*
>
> *- Norman Vincent Peale*

> *"If you do the right thing in front of the right people at the right place, at the right time, you'll be a success."*
>
> *- Duke Ellington*

Her letter, of course, made *my* day. It's always nice to know I've helped yet another individual through information I've gathered for publication. Every time I publish someone's name and address in my newsletter or a book, I can imagine someone else saying, "Now *this* is someone I've got to contact!"

On Keeping a Small Business Journal

Each of us working at home needs a few pats on the back from time to time but, often, we are the only ones to do this job. One way to boost your morale is to take time to look back on where you've been, so you'll know how far you've come in so short a time. I've found it helpful to document my progress in writing, through both written plans and goals and a small business diary. I urge you to do the same. Besides, you might want to write a book someday about how you succeeded in business, and your journal will provide an invaluable record.

When I began my business in 1981, I started such a journal, and as time passed, I found myself using it as a motivational tool. I could always look back six months or so and see from my journal notes that the things I worried about seldom happened, and that many of the goals I'd written months earlier were now being achieved. That realization always gave me a great deal of encouragement to keep pushing.

In a 1985 issue of *NHBR*, I shared a few of those notes to illustrate that even the most confident people have feelings of insecurity from time to time. I began my business with very little money and only two products: an $8 book and a $12/year newsletter. The odds for turning such small assets into a highly-profitable, self-supporting business were pretty slim. I thus had good reason to be concerned about every move I made, and I had to constantly rev myself up because, in the beginning, I was the only one who really believed it was possible. For example, one entry from my diary, November 29, 1981 reads:

> *"That mailing I was so worried about was a great success! I must remember to always trust my gut instinct, regardless of what others may tell me. And I MUST stop worrying so much! Things ARE going to work out for me. They always have—they always will. Worrying costs me energy I need for other things, and if I let it, it will age me sooner than necessary. I MUST have confidence. I WILL succeed. I need only keep working to achieve my personal and financial goals."*

Although I've got an enormous ego and am supremely self-confident, I still have moments of doubt when faced with a new challenge or experience; still have to screw up my courage to take new steps that involve financial risk; still get depressed once or twice a year over some aspect of my business...and still have to keep reminding myself that I WILL succeed at everything I do. So far, so good. Which brings me to one of my favorite quotes:"

> *If at first you do succeed,*
>
> *Try not to be INSUFFERABLE!*

"A book which has changed my life is Alan Lakein's How to Gain Control of Your Time and Your Life. He recommends making A, B, and C lists of things to do that will help you attain your lifetime goals. Then he suggests you throw away the B and C lists and concentrate on the A's, which are the ones you have decided are the most important.

"This idea has helped me a great deal in setting priorities and thinking about my activities. Then he suggests you figure out some 5-minute tasks you can do to work towards your goals. That may seem a rather unlikely way to go about it; after all, what can you do in five minutes? But it really works. If nothing else, you have made a small step towards your goal. At best, you may find yourself totally involved in the task for 30 minutes. This idea keeps me from wasting time on 'busy work' and focused on efficient tasks.

"My outline of this worthwhile book may be sketchy, but I give the author credit for helping me to overcome my procrastination habit."

— Donna Metcalfe, Owner
Good Scents

INSPIRATIONAL
THOUGHTS . . . *from Dennis E. Hensley*

In order to avoid boredom and stay motivated, the self-employed business leader must maintain a stimulating and fascinating life for himself or herself. Here are some ways in which I've found this can be accomplished:

● **Always be involved in some form of study.** Learning new things keeps the mind agile and stimulates creativity. So, register for a course in creating writing, sign up for a class in Chinese cooking or go to the library and check out three books on time management. Continually challenge your mind to expand.

● **Regularly take calculated risks.** Break out of the comfort zone by setting your sales goals a little higher than usual, by promising delivery dates a little earlier than is routine, or by moving into a sales territory you've previously avoided. Don't allow yourself to become casual about life or business. Complacency can be numbing.

● **Keep physically fit.** If you are coping with boredom by snacking, substitute games or exercise for food.

● **Schedule a private pep rally.** Try to arrange a free hour a few times each week so that you can listen to motivational tapes or view motivational video presentations. Not only will you learn some new and important business concepts, you'll also rekindle your competitive fires.

● **Try a change-of-pace activity.** Attend a weekend film festival, try go-carting, tour a doll museum, eat at an East Indian restaurant, or visit a wildlife preserve. There's a fascinating world out there waiting to be discovered.

Boredom, like failure, is self-inflicted. It is an avoidable emotional state. The enthusiastic business leader *will* avoid it.

To succeed as a homebased business operator, you need to be creative and innovative in everything from advertising to product development. Among the techniques and procedures that I have found most creative thinkers to rely upon are these:

● **The ability to go against the grain.** All successful thinkers contemplate radical thoughts. Daring to ask the nontraditional question leads the thinker to the next step, which is to discover how to make the impossible possible. This leads to new areas of investigation, new questions to ask. And that's creativity.

● **Overcoming the fear of making a mistake.** The only people who never make mistakes are the people who never try anything. Successful creative thinkers are so enthusiastic about finding an answer that they aren't thrown off by temporary setbacks. In fact, for many of them, trial and error is the most enjoyable part of the creative process.

● **Brainstorm the illogical.** With no limitations on his or her thinking, the creative person looks at existing practices and tries to imagine how they might be changed.

● **Mix apples and oranges.** Creative thinkers are nosy. They are always snooping into other people's professions to see what they can adapt to their own. They try other jobs, read books in professional fields other than their own, attend seminars on off-beat subjects, and strike up conversations with experts in numerous professionals. Many times, creative thinkers discover an innovation in one field that can be modified slightly to solve a problem in a different area.

Creative borrowing has been going on for ages. Truly creative thinkers put no blinders on their research. And since you, too, need to be creative, neither should you.

Dr. Hensley is the author of many inspirational books for business owners, writers and others, including Become Famous, Then Rich ($6.95 ppd.) and Uncommon Sense: Fueling Success Skills with Enthusiasm. Be sure to get acquainted with this excellent, motivational writer.

POSITIVE POETIC THOUGHTS

from Connie Hunt

SAYING NO

In the course of my life
I've been forced to say no
In every conceivable way.
NO, I'm busy, I'm out of touch.

No, I couldn't help you that much
I've gone back to school you see
To seek what I was meant to be.

I've taken a job
working six hours a day,
How could I possibly
Plan that luncheon in May?

I've children to drive
And a husband to feed.
Surely you can find
Someone else more in need
Of helping the church...
Community, scouts...

I'm finding myself,
Which leaves me out.

Oh, it has been a trying time
Fighting other's demands
Myself to find.

But if my NO causes distress
Please remember...
I'm not saying no to you
But to myself YES!

SAYING YES

In the course of my life
I have often said yes
with a resigned sigh.

Saying yes, you see, usually
implicates me in something
I wouldn't normally try.

But I must say this
that without some risk
I would never be
Who I am today.

For each "yes" brought me
an opportunity
to view life in a new way.

Though at times, a straight "no"
can save vertigo,
I have been most blest
by the times I've said "yes."

An excerpt from Reaching, by Connie Hunt. Reprinted by permission. Copyright 1983 by Connie Hunt.

Connie Hunt has has published two books of poetry; Reaching, a philosophical work, and Listening:An Inner Journey, "a personal journey into the stillness of self." Her address is in the resource chapter if you'd like to receive more information about either book.

The Power of Your Subconscious Mind

I know you're well aware of the power of positive thinking and the many business books that emphasize how to take control of your life or business through a change of mental attitude. Too few people, however, have fully developed the power of their subconscious mind, which can be one's strongest ally in times of trouble. Let me reemphasize that the subconscious mind has the ability to accept as real any impression that reaches it, whether negative or positive, constructive or destructive, reliable or unreliable. That's why it's so important to condition your mind to seek circumstances and things that are desired, while protecting it from undesirable influences and suggestions. Or, as Dale Carnegie put it: "Believe that you will succeed. Believe firmly, and you will then do what is necessary to bring success about."

In training my subconscious, I have always commanded myself, both verbally and in writing, to do certain things: be confident; think positively; believe in myself; trust my instincts, etc., and then I've followed through accordingly. I honestly believe I have succeeded *because* I commanded myself to succeed. That command—always in the forefront of my subconscious mind—is what I remember at each new juncture in my business. I ask myself, "If I'm going to succeed at this, what must I do to insure success?" And then my past business experience, coupled with a lifetime of living and plain common sense, all come together to give me the answer I need.

Through the years, I've learned that small miracles are always possible; that "spells of depression" come with the territory when you're in business, but can be defeated with a bit of effort; that financial worries are part of the game, and can be overcome; that your 'gut instinct' may be your most important business guide; that a positive attitude can make all the difference in the world; and that you will do exactly what you command yourself to do...now and in the future.

If you want to enjoy maximum success in your business, it's important that you continue to fill your conscious mind with new information and visions because the mind is like a giant computer that sees everything and forgets nothing. All you have to do is learn how to program it to work for you, so you can pull out the right information at the right time. This takes a little practice, but it's worth the effort. The more input you give your computer-like mind, the more new ideas and help it will give back to you. It will even solve your business problems for you, as I've happily learned from experience.

Not long ago, I was presented with a peculiar problem related to using my database software. My free support from the manufacturer had ended, no one at the computer store could solve my problem, and I couldn't find the answer in any of the reference books on my shelf. For a whole day, I pondered the problem, worried about it, and had trouble going to sleep that night because I knew I was in trouble if I didn't figure this out. Voila! On awakening the next morning, I had the answer. I had dreamed it—courtesy of my subconscious mind working on my behalf, of course. I sat down at the keyboard, did what my dream prompted me to do, and resolved the problem. I was absolutely elated to have yet another example of how my subconscious mind was working for me. These days, whenever I'm trying to figure out something, I firmly plant the question or problem in my mind just before going to bed, and often awake with "brilliant brainstorms." Try it; it works!

The Magic of Believing

"Women are supreme egotists—in the sense that when they get the idea they can do something, and that idea becomes thoroughly imbedded in their consciousness, they will stop at nothing to achieve their purpose.

"Even though Napoleon declared that he made circumstances, most men are its victims, while women by their very nature of thinking make circumstances serve them."

- from The Magic of Believing, *by Claude Bristol (Pocket Books)*

On Confidence

"One of the reasons I'm so confident isn't because I know I can handle everything well, but because I know I can clean up the mess," says Donna Munn, a Seattle area businesswoman.

"Confidence is being flexible enough to understand your own weaknesses, and being connected enough to go back and fix up whatever you can do, to acknowledge you're not right, to face the reality of situations.

"Confidence usually sneaks up on you. You've been pretending, practicing at seeing the vision of confidence, and one day you look at yourself and, hot diggity, you're confident. It's connected — and it's effortless."

- from a newspaper article in News Journal, Seattle.

Five Ways to
Stay Motivated

by Barbara Winter

● *Find an entrepre-
neurial friend—several, if
possible. They can fill a
gap in your life that no one
else can fill.*

● *Dress for the job.
Don't give in to the
temptation to shlep around in
your old bathrobe. Costume
yourself for the work to be
done. If I'm feeling like a
serious writer, I put on
jeans and a sweater; if my
duties are mostly
secretarial, I wear a skirt
and blouse; if there are
client calls to make, I dress
like a tycoon.*

● *Play music while you
work, if it doesn't distract
you. Like wearing the right
costume, the right music can
help set the stage for the
work you're doing.*

● *Give yourself a break.
Being your own boss can lead
to nonstop work. (The
world's worst slavedriver
would probably be less
demanding.) Take a walk,
write a letter to a friend,
listen to motivational
tapes. Schedule a break to
run errands in the middle of
your day. It can be refreshing and you'll accomplish
more.*

● *Take field trips.
Visit a successful business.
Or go to the library. Take a
seminar, or stroll through a
shopping mall. A different
setting, even for a few
hours, can recharge your
batteries and give you a
lift.*

Stretching Your Mind

During lunch with my students a few years ago at one of my workshops, a young woman of about 20 bombarded me with questions for which I had all kinds of answers. She asked, with a touch of humor in her voice, "How did you get to be so smart?", and I recall answering, "My dear, I'm almost 50 years old. It comes with the territory."

It comes, of course, if you've applied yourself to the fullest extent possible throughout your life. It's never too late to get rolling though. For proof, I need point only to my dear mother, who, at the age of 48 had to find an easier and better-paying job as my father could no longer work due to illness. In time, she decided to become an LPN, even though she was told she was almost too old to be accepted in this field. She went on to graduate at the top of her class and worked as an LPN well beyond the time she could have retired.

I recall her saying, about a year before the nursing challenge came, that she feared she was getting senile since she couldn't remember a thing. The trouble was, she had no special goals in life and her mind was not sufficiently stimulated at that time. What she went on to learn—and accomplish—staggers my mind. If there's one thing I don't want to hear from any of my readers, it's "...but I'm too old to learn all these new things or really do anything about my homebased business." Nonsense! Your body may be aging, but your mind will stay young so long as you keep it stimulated with new ideas and challenges. A lot of successful part-time businesses are being run by people over the age of 65.

Looking On The Bright Side

Most people get though life, I'm convinced, simply because they have a sense of humor. And when you work for yourself at home, it's essential for survival. I'm fortunate in that I married a man who always manages to find the humor in any situation. For example, it was raining when my first large shipment of *Homemade Money* was delivered, and, sure enough, it also rained a few months later when we took delivery on a large shipment of *Creative Cash*. As I watched Harry make a dozen trips back and and forth to the waiting truck on the street, hauling handtruck-loads of wet book boxes, I heard the truck driver ask, "Do you get shipments like this often?" "No," said a very wet Harry. "Only when it rains."

I also got a great laugh another day when I asked Harry what he had learned since I'd gotten him so involved in my business. Straightfaced, he replied, "I've learned how to spell Poughkeepsie, Albuquerque, Schenectady and Cucamonga."

To fully appreciate that remark, you need to know that Harry's job has always been handling routine mail and filling orders, which involves a considerable amount of typing, from order forms to address labels. As a retired professional musician, the last thing he ever expected to be doing in his "later years" was pounding out addresses on a typewriter, so naturally he never learned to type.

When the business grew to the point where I could no longer handle the mail myself, he volunteered to help, saying he could hunt-and-peck-out the names on our portable typewriter. Well, that typewriter has really gotten a workout ever since, and although Harry has never taken the time to learn how to type in the traditional manner, he has developed surprising speed with his own creative system. I call him my "three-finger-two-thumb wonder" because he actually uses both thumbs when he types. Never saw anything like it. And he almost never makes a typo error. Helpers like Harry are hard to come by these days. If you're lucky, you've got a humorous spouse to help cheer you up when you're down...and give you a hand with the business when it takes off. Maybe he'll even help keep your ego under control as you grow more successful.

I love to see my name in print, but I have to be careful not to let all this publicity or my fan mail go to my head. Not to worry—Harry helps me keep my head on straight with his humorous putdowns. One of my all-time favorites is the remark he made when I told him there once was a Saint who bore my name.

"Did you know that Saint Barbara was patron Saint to the artillery?" I asked in all seriousness.

"No," he replied, "but that explains why you think you're such a big shot."

Three Lists...Just For Fun

Awhile back, just for fun, I started a list that you might try too. It begins, I KNEW I WAS A SUCCESS WHEN...

● people began asking for my autograph

● other authors started interviewing me for their books

● I was able to get a line of credit on my signature only

● I started getting mail from American Express saying, "Your company has been recommended for the American Express Corporate Card."

● a feature story finally appeared on me in the newspaper published in Paxton, Illinois, the town NEXT to my home town of Buckley, which is too small for a paper of its own.

● My sister, Mary, told a friend that she ought to read my book, and her friend said, "You mean to say that YOU know Barbara Brabec?"

Along about that time, I also started another list: YOU'RE TOO BUSY WHEN...

● you're so busy you miss the eclipse of the sun.

● you don't even have time to collect the freebies offered by the Welcome Wagon hostess.

● You can't spare an hour for a free facial from the local Mary Kay gal.

● the only time your house gets cleaned is when company's coming.

● the only time your desk gets cleaned is when you spill a cup of coffee on it.

A mailing from the U. S. Department of Labor gave me a good laugh. I show it below for your amusement; note that not one address line is correct:

BARBARA BRABECK
NATL HORSE BASS REPORT
PO BOX 20137
UAPERVILLE IL 60566

Scene in one of Barbara's workshops where her home-business course was given for college credit:

BARBARA, TO YOUNG MAN: "What is your particular home-business interest, and what do you hope to gain from today's workshop?"

YOUNG MAN: "I don't have an interest in business. I'm just here because I need one credit to play hockey."

HOCKEY

Thoughts on Failure

Failure in one small business endeavor often gives us exactly what we need to succeed in another area— including such things as a new understanding and appreciation of our strengths and weaknesses, a better education in business basics, and a newfound knowledge of what works and what doesn't.

"Don't call it failure— call it growing," said a reader whose first business proved unprofitable. "If things had worked out for me the first time around, I probably wouldn't have gone on to other things which have proven more satisfying and profitable."

The above letter, and others like it eventually prompted this definition of success in my mind:

SUCCESS IS OFTEN FAILURE TURNED INSIDE OUT.

"I don't care what you do for a living. If you love it, you're a success. You don't have to be rich and famous. If you love what you're doing, you're successful whether you're making money or not."

- George Burns

For years, I honestly never knew how old I was at any given time because age simply didn't matter to me. Now I find myself wondering where the past 20 years have gone. With each passing year, I reflect upon the speed with which it flew by, and remind myself that I'm not getting any younger. Mentally, of course, I still feel about 25 years old. If only I could get my body to agree! Which brings me to my third list: YOU KNOW YOU'RE GETTING OLDER WHEN...

- you can't paste up your newsletter without magnifying glasses.

- you walk stiff-legged on ice, and worry about falling downstairs.

- you look at kids at play and wonder what it feels like to run like that.

- you spend a day pulling weeds and find yourself flat on your back that evening.

- you go to bed at 10:30 on New Year's Eve

- You begin to worry about losing everything you've worked so hard to get, and start putting your entire life in order.

Home Business Exercises

I blame my stressful working life for the fact that I've steadily gained weight since starting my present business. But of course I'm much too busy to start a regular exercise program and, besides, I spend most of each working day getting my own special brand of exercise (you, too, I'll bet):

```
* STRETCHING to reach new heights
  * LEAPING to grasp opportunity
    * RUNNING to meet deadlines
      * HOPPING from one project to another
        * STRUGGLING with responsibility
          * BEATING the bushes for new business
            * JUMPING to conclusions
              * FLYING off the handle
                * PULLING myself together...
                  * and PUSHING my luck!
```

As my publisher friend, Barbara Winter, says: "Life is wonderfully funny. Losers never learn that; winners never forget it. It's the best preventive medicine we've got."

So remember to take time now and then to congratulate yourself for a job well done, read uplifting books and periodicals to refresh your mind and spirits, and don't forget to look for the humor in your day-to-day business life. Small business owners may work a lot harder than the average employee, but at least they call the shots. Those of us who work at home are thankful to be in control of our own lives. For me, that thought alone makes all the blood, sweat and tears worthwhile. ▪▪

Resources

9.

How to Use This Resource Chapter

This chapter supplements the information in *Homemade Money—The Definitive Guide to Success in a Home Business*, which includes the most comprehensive and up-to-date directory of home-business/small business information resources in print—over 500 entries.

A code number in parentheses at the end of a listing is your clue that additional information is available to you by mail from the individual or company named. If a price is given, you may order at once by mail, although prices are always subject to change. The code, such as (A-II), (B-II), (G-II), etc. refers you to the complete address in section II, which is listed in alphabetical order.

Books & Directories

☐ *Cart Your Way to Success—A Peddler's Play in Three Acts*, by Gail Bird. A complete guide to selling in shopping malls with your own peddler's cart. $23.45 ppd. Free brochure. Birdhouse Enterprises. (B-II)

☐ *Catalog Marketing—The Complete Guide to Profitability in the Catalog Business*, by Katie Muldoon. (R.R. Bowker). In bookstores, $34.95.

☐ *Chase's Annual Events*. Annual publicity aid that lists special days, weeks and months of the year. Published by Contemporary Books. (B-II)

☐ *The College Newspaper Directory*. Enables advertisers to locate newspapers that accept paid ads. $6 ppd. from Lee Myers. (B-II)

☐ *Contracts for Artists*, by William Gignilliat. Includes many sample contracts useful to product sellers; consignment, commission, bill of sale, etc. $18.95 ppd. from Words of Art. (B-II)

☐ *Crafts Marketing Success Secrets*, by Barbara Brabec. A collection of the best information from the first three years of Barbara's newsletter when it was edited for craftsellers and known as *Sharing Barbara's Mail*. $11.45 ppd. from Barbara Brabec Productions. (B-II)

☐ *Creative Cash—Making Money with Your Crafts, Needlework, Designs & Know-How*. (Aames-Allen Pub.) The most popular crafts marketing guide in print—70,000+ copies sold! $13.95 ppd. from Barbara Brabec Productions. Free catalog details contents of this and author's other books and periodical. (B-II)

☐ *Directory of State Small Business Offices and Activities*. Most states have special small business assistance offices whose primary function is to give assistance to persons who wish to start a small business. The addresses of these state offices are found in this directory, free from the SBA's Office of Advocacy. (G-II)

☑ *Designing Greeting Cards and Paper Products*, by Ron Lister. (Spectrum/Prentice-Hall, 1984). Includes useful marketing tips. Check library.

☐ *Directory of Wholesale Reps*. A listing of 34 reps or rep agencies interested in hearing from professional craft producers. $5 ppd. from Northwoods Trading. (B-II)

☐ *Fifty Billion Dollar Directory*, and other directories for serious mail order sellers. Request more information from International Marketing Co., Inc. (B-II)

Guerrilla Marketing—Secrets for Making Big Profits From Your Small Business, by Jay Conrad Levinson. (Houghton Mifflin). $14.95. Highly recommended to business owners willing to "go the distance." Check bookstores or write Houghton Mifflin to order by mail. (B-II)

Homemade Money — The Definitive Guide to Success in a Homebased Business, by Barbara Brabec. Revised/expanded 1989 ed., $18.95 ppd. from Barbara Brabec Prod. Free catalog. (B-II)

How to Borrow Money From a Bank, by Don H. Alexander. A non-technical guide that explains how bankers think, and what kind of "paper" they want to see from loan applicants. $6.95 ppd. from DHA & Assoc. (B-II)

Start Your Own AT-Home Day Care Center, by Patricia Gallagher (Doubleday). Contact the author for price and availability of this and other day care how-to guides she has written. (A-II)

Ideas That Work—10 of Today's Most Exciting and Profitable Self-Employment Opportunities, by Susan Elliott. (Live Oak). Covers child care, household services, word-processing, catering, writing, editing, publishing, image consulting, teaching and lawn & garden services. $10.95 ppd. from New Careers Center. Send $1 to receive an excellent "Whole Work Catalog" of the best small business books available by mail. (B-II)

Kids Mean Business, by Barbralu Manning. (Live Oak). How to turn a love of children into a profitable homebased business. (Covers toy shops, daycare centers, day camps, children's clothing boutiques, writing kids' books, & teaching of all kinds. $10.95 ppd. from The New Careers Center. (B-II)

Julian Block's Guide to Year-Round Tax Savings. (Prentice-Hall). Regularly updated; Available in bookstores. (A-II)

Management Workbooks for Self-Employed People. A free brochure detailing the five books in this series is available from Dodd-Blair & Associates. (A-II)

Money Making Marketing, by Jeffrey Lant. $32.50 ppd. If you're serious about your business, be sure to read this book. Lots of "trade secrets" in it! (See also "Unabashed Self-Promoter" listing below to order author's catalog.) (B-II)

The Publicity Manual by Kate Kelly. An invaluable aid for anyone who's serious about getting publicity. $29.95 ppd. from the author. (A-II)

Settle It Yourself—Who Needs a Lawyer, by Dorothea Kaplan and Fred Benjamin. Forms and letters you need, in usable formats, for a quick settlement. $11.95 ppd. from D. Kaplan. (A-II)

Small-Time Operator—How to Start Your Own Business, Keep Your Books, Pay Your Taxes, and Stay Out of Trouble, by Bernard Kamoroff. The best book of its kind you'll ever find! Regularly updated. Request order form from Bell Springs Publishing. (B-II)

That's a Great Idea! by Husch & Foust. (Ten Speed Press). An excellent guidebook for anyone who's trying to develop, protect or sell new product ideas. Available in bookstores and libraries. (B-II)

Totally Organized, by Bonnie McCullough. (St. Martin's Press). Workable systems for personal and home organization that will make your home-business life run more smoothly as well. $12.45 ppd. from the author. (A-II)

The Unabashed Self-Promoter's Guide by Jeffrey Lant. $32.50 ppd. One of several helpful business books by this author. Be sure to request his free "Sure-Fire Business Success Catalog." (B-II)

Working From Home—Is It For You? by William Atkinson. (Dow Jones-Irwin). Includes chapters on self-management, psychological and historical perspectives of the work-at-home movement. Another good book that's been allowed to go out of print; check your library. (B-II)

Your Ideas May Be Worth A Fortune, by Woodie Hall. Loaded with wit, marketing wisdom and solid how-to guidelines for success. $20 ppd. from Mark Nolan Associates. (A-II)

Periodicals

Bed & Breakfast Update. Bimonthly newsletter companion to Beverly Mathews' popular book on the same topic. It condenses the latest info on B&B from over 100 sources. Free brochure. (P-II)

Classified Communication. This informative newsletter is published to help advertisers write better ads and acquaint them with the various publications in the Rodale Press family. Request a copy, mentioning this book. (P-II)

☐ *DM News*. This trade paper is distributed free of charge to qualified direct marketers, and it keeps mailers up to date on everything happening in the direct response industry. Request a subscription on your mail-oriented business letterhead. (P-II)

☐ *FAWN Update*. Newsletter devoted to minority and women entrepreneurs. (P-II)

☐ *Freebies Magazine*. A lot of small businesses have received publicity in this consumer publication. So can you. Ask magazine for it's "business publicity package." (P-II)

☑ *Gifts & Decorative Accessories*. A monthly magazine for retailers but helpful to anyone in the gifts industry. Subscription includes a supply source directory. Request subscription information on business letterhead. (P-II)

☐ *National Home Business Report*. Quarterly companion to this and other books by Barbara Brabec. $18/yr.U.S.; $22/year Foreign (U.S. Funds). Sample back issue, $4 ppd. from Barbara Brabec. (P-II)

☐ *Opportunity Magazine*. Readers of this monthly include independent salesmen, party plan operators, distributors, jobbers and others who sell to a variety of retail/wholesale outlets. (P-II)

☐ *Sew It Seams*. Directed to both professional and non-professional seamstresses, each issue includes a profile of someone who is successfully operating a sewing business. Sample, $4. (P-II)

☐ *Sharing Ideas Newsmagazine*. This is an essential resource for those who speak to promote their business, or are paid to speak. Edited by Dottie Walters, who also runs a speaking bureau. Ask for complete information. (P-II)

☑ *Shoestring Marketer Newsletter*. Published monthly for small business owners. Also from this source: *Getting a Good Start in a Mailing Services Business*. $6 ppd. (P-II)

☐ *Tax Hotline Newsletter*. Keeps readers up to date on the latest tax law changes and how they affect small business. (P-II)

☐ *Winning Ways News*. A motivational newsletter that emphasizes personal growth and business how-to's. Edited by Barbara Winter. Send SASE for info. (P-II)

Organizations/Networks

☐ American Home Business Association. National organization that offers a newsletter, discounts on office supplies/equipment, insurance program, toll-free advisory service. For info, call toll-free: 1-800-433-6361, mentioning Barbara Brabec. (O-II)

☐ American Institute of Small Business. Offers entrepreneurial courses and manuals. (O-II)

☐ Business Entrepreneurs Exchange. A nonprofit organization designed to meet the needs of small business people in the Orange, California area. (O-II)

☐ *The Home Business Advocate*. Bimonthly newsletter for Canadian homebased business owners. Edited by Wendy Priesnitz. (P-II)

☐ Leads Club. A networking club for success-oriented women who want to increase their business. As of January '87, there were 174 chapters nationwide and 3,000 members. Write for information on how to start a Leads Club network in your area. (O-II)

☐ Mothers' Home Business Network. Membership in this network now exceeds 3,000, with members in each of the 50 states. Members receive the periodical, *Homeworking Mothers* and can participate in cooperative "Mothers' Mailpak" mailings. (O-II)

Other Business Information & Resources

☐ Article Reprint, "Good Contracts Reduce Stress and Cover Assets," $1 plus SASE. From Janet Oberndorfer. (A-II)

☐ *Arts Self-Publishing Kit*. Includes a copy of the directory mentioned on pg. 84, plus samples of all promotional pieces and advertising rate cards used by the publisher. $19.95 ppd. from Jack Mandel. (A-II)

☐ Books by Dennis Hensley. Send this author an SASE to receive information about his business and motivational books. (A-II)

☐ Books by Herman Holtz. Send this author an SASE to receive a listing of his most popular business books on mail order, consulting, computers, business writing, publishing, and more. (A-II)

☐ *Business Opportunities for Home Economists.* This booklet covers development of a career plan, goal setting and more. $2 ppd. from Home Economists in Business. (O-II)

☐ Calligraphic logos and artwork, designed by Sylvia Churchbaugh especially for your business, are turned into rubber stamps you can use in a variety of ways. SASE brings details. (S-II)

☐ Computers. *Putting Your PC To work At Home* is an 8-page guide describing the various options available. Includes a resource list of newsletters, associations and books for more information. $5 ppd. from Gil Gordon. (M-II)

☐ Consumer Product Safety Information. Request copies of the requirements for consumer product safety, use of hazardous substances, and the flammability standard from Consumer Products Safety Commission. (G-II)

☐ Copyright Information. Free information on all aspects of the copyright law is available from The Copyright Office. For information on how to make a search of the Copyright Office catalogs, or have the Copyright Office make a search for you, ask for Circular R22. (G-II)

☐ Craft Shop Directories. *A Guide to Creative Outlets* is $3 ppd.from The Country Press (B-II); *Annual Directory of Craft Shops* is $6 ppd. from The Front Room. (B-II).

☐ Federal Information Centers (FICS). FICS serve as a central point of contact for people with questions about the Federal Government and its services who have been unable to find answers elsewhere. A fact sheet and listing of FICS nationally is available on request. (G-II)

☐ *How to Save Money on Office Supplies.* A free booklet available from Quill Corporation. (S-II)

☐ IRA Kit. For information on how to start your own Individual Retirement Account, request this free kit from Strong Funds. (M-II)

☐ Labels. Something new! Self-adhesive, color labels from your own negatives. Four sizes, small minimum quantity. Great for packaging, sales materials, catalog sheets, reports, letters, etc. Free brochure from Photolabels. (S-II)

☐ Networking Literature. If you're still trying to figure out what "networking" is all about, here's a source for some good literature on the topic. The 64-page booklet, "The Networking Game" is $3 ppd.; for $1 you can get an article reprint about open networking. Write Pattern Research. (O-II)

☐ Party Plan Information. *A Guide to Marketing Crafts Through the Home Party System* is available for $5 ppd. from Village Vendor. (A-II)

☐ Postage Meters. Pitney Bowes will send you information about a variety of postage meters, including their electronic "Postage-by-Phone" meter system for low-volume mailers. Write or phone 1-800-MR BOWES, ext. 463. (S-II)

☐ Promotional Ideas aplenty are yours in the interesting "My Card" booklet published by Steve Winter, who offers more than 20 books, cassettes and other publications. Mention this book to receive this booklet for $1 from Living Skill Media. (M-II)

☐ Quilter's Business Information. Oliver Press publishes *The Professional Quilter* magazine, and four booklets—on pricing, shop start-up, slides and bookkeeping. An SASE will bring descriptive brochure. (B-II)

☐ Supply Catalogs. Call 1-800-421-1222 for a free "Office Supply Buyer's Guide" from Viking Office Products (S-II). * If you need boxes or packing supplies, request free catalog from U. S. Box Corporation (S-II). * For a wide assortment of graphic art supplies and equipment, send $1 for catalog from Dot Pasteup Supply. (S-II).

☐ Telephone marketing. Have they got your number...and do you want to stop those aggravating prerecorded advertising messages? You can get your name removed from such national calling lists by making a request to the Telephone Preference Service of The Direct Marketing Association. (O-II)

☐ *Thomas Register* Free Listing Form. If you sell to industrial accounts, you might want to be listed in this directory. Meanwhile, use it in the library to find virtually any product or service needed in your business. (S-II)

☐ Trademark Search Service. If you're willing to pay (about $100), Government Liaison Service will search a name for copyright or trademark and get back to you in a couple of days' time. The firm will also process your application for a trademark ($150) and virtually guarantee immediate processing. Write for more information. (G-II)

SECTION II

A Special Note About Individuals' Addresses

These have been included to facilitate an exchange of correspondence for networking or other business purposes. If you are engaged in a similar business activity, and believe it would be mutually beneficial to get acquainted with certain individuals who have contributed to this book, they would be pleased to hear from you. *Do not, however, write for the express purpose of asking questions.* Instead, look for the answers you need in books such as those listed in this chapter and in the resource chapter of *Homemade Money*.

NOTE: Numbers in parenthesis on line 1 of any address refer to page numbers in the book where the listee is mentioned editorially.

(A-II) - Authors & Contributors to this Book

Leila Albala (85, 89, 109)
ALPEL
P. O. Box 203
Chambly, Quebec, Canada J3L4B3

William Atkinson ((29)
P. O. Box "J"
Murphysboro, IL 62966

Steven Bennett (9)
S. J. Bennett & Co.
P. O. Box 1090
Cambridge, MA 02238

Carl Betz (88)
Glass Creations
1251 Glenbrook Rd.
Huntingdon Valley, PA 19006

Julian Block (53, 55)
3 Washington Square
Larchmont, NY 10538

Janet Brewer (104, 106)
JL Brewer Co.
41-A Lake Street
Wilmington, MA 01887

Joellen Buzinec (104)
JOBEE
4264 Colorado St. S.E.
Prior Lake, MN 55372

Donald W. Caudill (84)
University of North Alabama
P. O. Box 5039 UNA
Florence, AL 35632

Jan A. DeYoung (8, 39)
Iowa Small Business
   Development Centers
Chamberlynn Bldg., 137 Lynn
Ames, IA 50010

Gerry Dodd & Ann Blair (52)
Dodd-Blair & Associates
P. O. Box 269
Farmington, ME 04938

Margaret M. Feeney (96)
Mktg. Consultant, Maine
   Industrial Accounts
Thomas Register
51 Davis Street
South Portland, ME 04106

Patricia Gallagher
Child Care and You
Box 555
Worcester, PA 19490

Woodie Hall (87)
1325 El Corrall Lane
Lake San Marcos, CA 92069

Mary Hansen (103)
That's the Way!
P. O. Box 89
Markham, Ontario
Canada L3P 3J5

Lisa Gawne Hantzis (82)
Lisa People
767 North Center St.
San Pedro, CA 90731

Dennis Hensley (109, 113)
Denehen, Inc.
4316 Marvin Drive
Ft. Wayne, IN 46806

Linda Highley (80)
Highley Decorative
706 Esther Dr.
Arnold, MO 63010

Herman Holtz (78, 79, 101)
P. O. Box 1731
Wheaton, MD 20902

Connie Hunt (114)
Pulsar Publications
120 Village Square, Suite 117
Orinda, CA 94563

Dorothea Kaplan, J.D. (64)
Law Lab, Inc.
20 North Clark, Suite 2306
Chicago, IL 60602

Kate Kelly (105, 108)
Visibility Enterprises
11 Rockwood Drive
Larchmont, NY 10538

Eugene L. Larson (44)
Model Ship Marine
9223 Presidential Drive
Alexandria, VA 22309

Jack Mandel (84)
Island Craft & Bus.Consultants
360 Cameo Drive
Massapequa, NY 11758

Diane Lea Mathews (86)
The Herbal Kitchen
Box 134
Salisbury Center, NY 13454

Bonnie McCullough
P. O. Box 28086, #16
Lakewood, CO 80228

Nancy M. McFayden (99)
Gingham 'n Spice, Ltd.
4356 Biddeford Circle
Doylestown, PA 18901

Donna Metcalf (112)
Good Scents
P. O. Box 854
Rialto, CA 92376

Carol Rae Mowery (106)
RD 1, Box 1864
Nescopeck, PA 18635

Mary Mulari (72)
Mary's Productions
P. O. Box 87
Aurora, MN 55705

Janet Oberndorfer (33)
Lady Resourceful, Inc.
P. O. Box 7241
Garden City, NY 11530

Bob "Bush" Prisby (13, 17)
Prisby's Country
388 Ingomar Street
Pittsburgh, PA 15216

Roger Richman Productions, Inc. (67)
9777 Wilshire Blvd.
Los Angeles, CA 90069

Carol Saathoff (100
Creative Critters
E. 4240 Woodland Drive
Post Falls, ID 83854

Viv & Art Sloane (90)
Viv's Ribbons & Laces
212 Virginia Hills Drive
Martinez, CA 94553

Nancy Smeltzer (108)
Fiber Fantasies
9822 Pushcart Way
Columbia, MD 21045

Edwin Smith (98, 106)
Craftsmith
5760 W. 79th
Indianapolis, IN 46278

Bob Storey (13, 16)
Together Products
3720-32nd Ave. W.
Seattle, WA 98199

Village Vendor (104)
Marion Boyer & Jo Mucha
604 Calico
Portage, MI 49081

Susan Winchester (106)
Sweeter Measures
Rt. 1, Box 126-B
Gibbon, NE 68840

Kathy Wirth/Dianne Davis (68)
KD Artistry
800 Compton Rd., Suite 22
Cincinnati, OH 45231

(B-II) - Book Publishers and Related Resources

Bell Springs Publishing (54)
Attn: Bernard Kamoroff
P. O. Box 640
Laytonville, CA 95454

Barbara Brabec Productions (32)
P. O. Box 2137
Naperville, IL 60567

Birdhouse Enterprises
110 Jennings Avenue
Patchogue, NY 11772

Contemporary Books (103)
180 North Michigan Avenue
Chicago, IL 60601

The Country Press
Attn: Janet L. Walker
P. O. Box 5024
Durango, CO 81302

DHA & Associates
P. O. Box 1861
Seattle, WA 98111

The Front Room
P. O. Box 1541
Clifton, NJ 07015

Houghton Mifflin Co. (81)
2 Park Street
Boston, MA 02108

Int'l. Marketing Co., Inc.
Attn: Mervyn Heaton
17057 Bellflower Blvd.
Bellflower, CA 90706

Jeffrey Lant Associates (110)
Attn: Jeffrey Lant
50 Follen St., Suite 507
Cambridge, MA 02138

Lee Myers
5630 Wilson Rd., Ste. A
Bakersfield, CA 93309

Mosaic Press (28)
Attn: Miriam Irwin
358 Oliver Rd.
Cincinnati, OH 45215

National Register Publishing
    Co., Inc. (86)
3004 Glenview Road
Wilmette, IL 60091

The New Careers Center
Attn: Tom Ellison
Box 297
Boulder, CO 80306

Mark Nolan Associates
P. O. Box 2069
Citrus Heights, CA 95611

Northwoods Trading Company
Attn: Sharon Olson
13451 Essex Court
Eden Prairie, MN 55347

Oliver Press
Attn: Jeanie M. Spears
4414 Greenhaven Dr.
St. Paul, MN 55104

Prentice-Hall, Inc. (101)
Englewood Cliffs, NJ 07632

Public Relations Publishing
   Co., Inc. (102)
888 7th Avenue
New York, NY 10106

Rocky Point Press
P. O. Box 4814
North Hollywood, CA 91607

Words of Art, Inc.
Box 2
Atlanta, GA 30301

(G-II) - Government Resources

The Consumer Products Safety
   Commission (69)
Bureau of Compliance
5401 Westbard Ave.
Bethesda, MD 20207

The Copyright Office (71, 73)
Library of Congress
Washington, DC 20559

Federal Information Ctrs. (38,71)
Consumer Information Center
Dept. 587M
Pueblo, CO 81009

Government Liaison Svcs.Inc. (72)
Suite 108, Washington Bldg.
3030 Claredon Blvd.
Arlington, VA 22201

U. S. Small Business
   Administration (7-10)
Office of Advocacy
1441 "L" St., N.W.
Washington, DC 20416

(M-II) -Other Business and Marketing Connections

Aggressive List Management (86)
3231 N. Frontage Rd., Suite 3111
Arlington Heights, IL 60004

Gil Gordon Associates
Attn: Gil Gordon
10 Donner Court
Monmouth Junction, NJ 08852

Jefferson Institute of
   Financial Independence (56)
757 South Main
Springville, UT 84663

Living Skill Media
Attn: Steve Winter
1497-1/2 Queen St. West 71
Toronto, Canada M6R 1A3

Strong Funds (57)
Attn: Bruce Behling, V.P.
815 East Mason Street
Milwaukee, WI 53202

(O-II) Organizations/Networks

The American Association for
   State and Local History (86)
172 2nd Ave., Suite 102
Nashville, TN 37201

The American Association of
   Museums (86)
1225 Eye St., NW, Suite 200
Washington, DC 20005

American Home Business Association
397 Post Road
Darien, CT 06820

American Institute of Small
   Business (27)
Max Fallek, President
7515 Wayzata Blvd., Suite 201
Minneapolis, MN 55426

Business Entrepreneurs Exchange
David Simpson, Director
P. O. Box 6232
Orange, CA 92613

Direct Marketing Assn. (37)
6 E. 43rd St.
New York, NY 10017

Direct Selling Education
   Foundation (37)
1776 "K" St., N.W., Suite 600
Washington, DC 20006

Home Economists in Business
5008 Pine Creek Dr., Suite B
Westerville, OH 43081

Inventors Workshop International
   Educational Foundation (82)
P. O. Box 251
Tarzana, CA 91356

Leads Club
Ali Lassen, Founder
P. O. Box 24
Carlsbad, CA 92008

Midwest Entrepreneurial Assn.
Attn: Bob Miller
P. O. Box 766
Bloomington, IL 61702

Mothers' Home Business Network
Attn: Georganne Fiumara
P. O. Box 423
East Meadow, NY 11554

National Association for the
    Self-Employed (35)
2324 Gravel Rd.
Ft. Worth, TX 76118

Pattern Research
P. O. Box 9845
Denver, CO 80209

Periodical Publishers

Classified Communications (93)
Attn: Linda Bancroft
Rodale Press
33 E. Minor St.
Emmaus, PA 18049

Bed & Breakfast Update
P. O. Box 4814
North Hollywood, CA 91607

Crafts Plus (85)
Box 427
Unionville, Ontario
Canada L3R 5V1

DM News (93)
10 Olympia Lane
Stony Brook, NY 11790

FAWN Update
P. O. Box 14411
Chicago, IL 60614

Freebies Magazine
P. O. Box 20283
Santa Barbara, CA 93120

Gifts & Decorative Access. (100)
51 Madison Avenue
New York, NY 10010

Hands Magazine (85)
P. O. Box 340, Station L
Toronto, Ont. Canada M6E 4Z2

The Home Business Advocate
195 Markville Rd.
Unionville, Ont.Canada L3R 4V8

In Business (7)
Box 323
Emmaus, PA 18049

National Flea Market Dealer (9)
11565 Ridgewood Circle No.
Seminole, FL 33542

National Home Business Report (5)
P. O. Box 2137
Naperville, IL 60567

Opportunity Magazine (91)
6 North Michigan Ave., Suite 1405
Chicago, IL 60602

Sew It Seams
P. O. Box 2698
Kirkland, WA 98083

Sharing Ideas Newsmagazine (47)
P. O. Box 1120
Glendora, CA 91740

Shoestring Marketer News-
    letter (59)
P. O. Box 1389
Yuba City, CA 95992

Ruff Times (15)
Target, Inc.
P. O. Box 25
Pleasanton, CA 94566

Tax Hotline Newsletter (54)
330 W. 42nd St.
New York, NY 10036

Winning Ways (26)
P. O. Box 35412
Minneapolis, MN 55435

(S-II) Suppliers

Brookstone Co. (38)
127 Vose Farm Rd.
Peterborough, NH 03458

Sylvia Churchbaugh
8010 Conser, Box 4001
Overland Park, KS 66204

Dot Pasteup Supply Co.
1612 California St.
P. O. Box 369
Omaha, NE 68101

Photolabels (USA) Inc.
333 Kimberly Drive
Carol Stream, IL 60188

Pitney Bowes (37)
Attn: Sally A. Scudo
Location 55-13
Stamford, CT 06926

Quill Corporation (78)
100 S. Schelter Rd., Box 464A
Lincolnshire, IL 60069

Thomas Register
Thomas Publishing Company
One Penn Plaza
New York, NY 10001

U. S. Box Corporation
1298 McCarter Highway
Newark, NJ 07104

Viking Office Products, Inc.
P. O. Box 465644
Cincinnati, OH 45246

Index